Saturday's Children

Edited by Helen Plotz

THOMAS Y. CROWELL CO.

The Earth Is the Lord's
Poems of the Spirit

Imagination's Other Place
Poems of Science and Mathematics

Poems from the German

Poems of Emily Dickinson

Poems of Robert Louis Stevenson

Untune the Sky
Poems of Music and the Dance

The Marvelous Light
Poets and Poetry

MACMILLAN PUBLISHING CO., INC.

The Pinnacled Tower
Selected Poems of Thomas Hardy

GREENWILLOW BOOKS

As I Walked Out One Evening
A Book of Ballads

The Gift Outright
America to Her Poets

Life Hungers to Abound
Poems of the Family

This Powerful Rhyme
A Book of Sonnets

Gladly Learn and Gladly Teach
Poems of the School Experience

Saturday's Children
Poems of Work

Saturday's Children

Poems of Work
Chosen by HELEN PLOTZ

GREENWILLOW BOOKS • New York

Copyright © 1982 by Helen Plotz

The Acknowledgments on pages 171–174
constitute an extension of the copyright page.

Library of Congress Cataloging in Publication Data

Main entry under title:
Saturday's children.
Summary: An anthology of more than 100 poems
from all over the world on the subject of work.
1. Labor and laboring classes—Juvenile poetry.
2. Children's poetry.   [1. Labor and laboring
classes—Poetry.   2. Poetry—Collections]
I. Plotz, Helen.   PN6110.L15S2
808.81'9355   82-3087
ISBN 0-688-01406-2   AACR2

In memory of Milton
and for the newest members of our family,
John's wife, Suzanna Yeh,
and their son
David Chu-Phai

Contents

Introduction

"And God saw everything that he had made, and, behold it was very good. And on the seventh day God ended his work which he had made; and he rested on the seventh day from all his work which he had made." Such is the joy of work. And this is the sorrow of work: "In the sweat of thy face shalt thou eat bread."

These two opposing attitudes toward work are with us still. We rejoice in work and we describe it as a burden often in almost the same breath. Is work a blessing or a curse? This is a question which cannot be answered but only clumsily explained. We can gather definitions of the joy and the sorrow from our literature and our experience. In this collection of poems we will see both attitudes. I have tried to convey my belief in the importance and necessity of work in these poems which range from Bible times to the present, and I have included nursery rhymes and popular songs as well as serious verse of great beauty.

That ambivalence reigns in our attitude toward work is made clear in popular sayings such as "All work and no play makes Jack a dull boy" and the different adage "Satan finds some mischief still for idle hands to do."

Much literature not directly concerned with work uses images of work to strengthen its theme. Shakespeare's "dyer's hand," the Bible's "eye of the needle," Longfellow's "mills of God," and Hopkins's "all trades, their gear and tackle and trim" are examples of this. There are words that we use constantly whose origins are in the world of work. A few of these are: plant, harvest, dye, reap, spin, weave, mend. For example, we may say, "I have planted a certain idea," or, "You must mend your ways." It would be interesting to think about such words and to discover how they became part of our everyday

[xi]

language. There are also surnames derived from occupations. Some of these are Taylor, Clark, Farmer, Smith, Carter, and Hunter. There are many others.

The joy of working at one's true vocation can be destroyed by unemployment or by being forced into a deadly routine. Incidentally, I should like to emphasize that housework and other nonintellectual occupations are not menial or meaningless and that white is not inherently superior to blue as a color for a collar. Interpretations of the meaning of all labor, of its tragedy and of its comedy have been movingly portrayed by many poets.

The wretchedness of child labor has been going on for many years and in certain parts of the world is still going on. Children have died on their jobs and have been handicapped as a result of their jobs. Being opposed to child labor does not, of course, imply that children must not work at household or neighborhood chores. On the contrary, we know that learning to work early in life is the best preparation for a happy and successful adult life.

The phrase "working class" is frequently used and I'm not sure that I know its meaning. Its popular definition is, of course, a description of a group of people who are poorer and less educated than so-called middle- and upper-class people, and who are engaged in occupations that are physically but not mentally demanding. We should think about this and ask ourselves whether we want to perpetuate these clichés or whether we can learn to accept all work as valuable and necessary. I hasten to add that there are many people who believe that artists, writers, and scholars don't do real work. These generalizations about "work" work both ways.

The first section, "When Adam Delved," consists of poems of the rural occupations.

The second section, "Let Her Own Work Praise Her," contains poems of women's work of every kind.

The third section, "A Long Way We Come; a Long Way to Go," which is made up of poems of child labor and work in mines and factories, is given to industrial work and includes the disaster of unemployment.

The last section, "What a Prodigious Step to Have Taken," is a selection of poems on work as a calling and the fulfillment or the frustration that it brings. It also includes children's poems which tell us how vocations appear to them as they look into the puzzling world of grown-ups.

Let us begin with a poem by W. H. Auden which praises "the prodigious steps" of "nameless heroes" and conveys the spirit of this gathering of verse.

from Horae Canonicae

SEXT

You need not see what someone is doing
to know if it is his vocation,

you have only to watch his eyes:
a cook mixing a sauce, a surgeon

making a primary incision,
a clerk completing a bill of lading,

wear the same rapt expression,
forgetting themselves in a function.

How beautiful it is,
that eye-on-the-object look.

To ignore the appetitive goddesses,
to desert the formidable shrines

of Rhea, Aphrodite, Demeter, Diana,
to pray instead to St. Phocas,

St. Barbara, San Saturnino,
or whoever one's patron is,

that one may be worthy of their mystery,
what a prodigious step to have taken.

There should be monuments, there should be odes,
to the nameless heroes who took it first,

to the first flaker of flints
who forgot his dinner,

the first collector of sea-shells
to remain celibate.

Where should we be but for them?
Feral still, un-housetrained, still

wandering through forests without
a consonant to our names,

slaves of Dame Kind, lacking
all notion of a city,

and, at this noon, for this death,
there would be no agents.

W. H. AUDEN

When Adam Delved

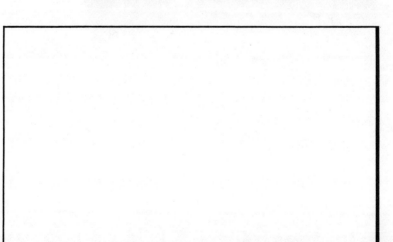

When Adam Delved

When Adam delved and Eve span
Who was then a gentleman?

Text used by John Ball in his speech at Blackheath to the men in Wat Tyler's rebellion (1381). John Ball, an English priest who took part in the insurrection, was executed at St. Albans in June of that year.—H. P.

The Man with the Hoe

(Written after seeing Millet's world-famous painting*)

Bowed by the weight of centuries he leans
Upon his hoe and gazes on the ground,
The emptiness of ages in his face,
And on his back the burden of the world.
Who made him dead to rapture and despair,
A thing that grieves not and that never hopes,
Stolid and stunned, a brother to the ox?
Who loosened and let down this brutal jaw?
Whose was the hand that slanted back this brow?
Whose breath blew out the light within this brain?

Is this the Thing the Lord God made and gave
To have dominion over sea and land;
To trace the stars and search the heavens for power;
To feel the passion of Eternity?
Is this the dream He dreamed who shaped the suns
And marked their ways upon the ancient deep?
Down all the caverns of Hell to their last gulf
There is no shape more terrible than this—
More tongued with censure of the world's blind greed—
More filled with signs and portent for the soul—
More packt with danger to the universe.

What gulfs between him and the seraphim!
Slave of the wheel of labor, what to him
Are Plato and the swing of Pleiades?
What the long reaches of the peaks of song,
The rift of dawn, the reddening of the rose?
Through this dread shape the suffering ages look;
Time's tragedy is in that aching stoop;
Through this dread shape humanity betrayed,
Plundered, profaned, and disinherited,
Cries protest to the Judges of the World,
A protest that is also prophecy.

[4]

O masters, lords and rulers in all lands,
Is this the handiwork you give to God,
This monstrous thing distorted and soul-quenched?
How will you ever straighten up this shape;
Touch it again with immortality;
Give back the upward looking and the light;
Rebuild in it the music and the dream;
Make right the immemorial infamies,
Perfidious wrongs, immedicable woes?

O masters, lords and rulers in all lands,
How will the Future reckon with this man?
How answer his brute question in that hour
When whirlwinds of rebellion shake all shores?
How will it be with kingdoms and with kings—
With those who shaped him to the thing he is—
When this dumb terror shall rise to judge the world,
After the silence of the centuries?

EDWIN MARKHAM

* *"As I looked at Millet's* The Man with the Hoe, *I realized that I was looking on no mere man of the field; but was looking on a plundered peasant, typifying the millions left over as the debris from the thousand wars of the masters and from their long industrial oppressions, extending over the ages. This Hoe-man might be a stooped consumptive toiler in a New York City sweat-shop; a man with a pick, spending nearly all his days underground in a West Virginia coal mine; a man with a labor-broken body carrying a hod in a London street; a boatman with strained arms and aching back rowing for hours against the heavy current of the Volga."—E. M.*

The Lay of the Labourer

A spade! a rake! a hoe!
  A pickaxe, or a bill!
A hook to reap, or a scythe to mow,
  A flail, or what ye will—
And here's a ready hand
  To ply the needful tool,
And skill'd enough, by lessons rough,
  In Labour's rugged school.

To hedge, or dig the ditch,
  To lop or fell the tree,
To lay the swarth on the sultry field,
  Or plough the stubborn lea;
The harvest stack to bind,
  The wheaten rick to thatch,
And never fear in my pouch to find
  The tinder or the match.

To a flaming barn or farm
  My fancies never roam;
The fire I yearn to kindle and burn
  Is on the hearth of Home;
Where children huddle and crouch
  Through dark long winter days,
Where starving children huddle and crouch,
  To see the cheerful rays,
A-glowing on the haggard cheek,
  And not in the haggard's blaze!

To Him who sends a drought
  To parch the fields forlorn,
The rain to flood the meadows with mud.
  The lights to blast the corn,
To Him I leave to guide
  The bolt in its crooked path.
To strike the miser's rick, and show
  The skies blood-red with wrath.

[6]

A spade! a rake! a hoe!
  A pickaxe, or a bill!
A hook to reap, or a scythe to mow,
  A flail, or what ye will—
The corn to thrash, or the hedge to plash,
  The market-team to drive,
Or mend the fence by the cover side,
  And leave the game alive.

Ay, only give me work,
  And then you need not fear
That I shall snare his worship's hare,
  Or kill his grace's deer;
Break into his lordship's house,
  To steal the plate so rich;
Or leave the yeoman that had a purse
  To welter in a ditch.

Wherever Nature needs
  Wherever Labour calls,
No job I'll shirk of the hardest work,
  To shun the workhouse walls;
Where savage laws begrudge
  The pauper babe its breath,
And doom a wife to a widow's life,
  Before her partner's death.

My only claim is this,
  With labour stiff and stark,
By lawful turn, my living to earn,
  Between the light and dark;
My daily bread, and nightly bed,
  My bacon, and drop of beer—
But all from the hand that holds the land,
  And none from the overseer!

No parish money, or loaf,
  No pauper badges for me,
A son of the soil, by right of toil
  Entitled to my fee.
No alms I ask, give me my task:
  Here are the arm, the leg,
The strength, the sinews of a Man,
  To work, and not to beg.

Still one of Adam's heirs,
  Though doom'd by chance of birth
To dress so mean, and to eat the lean
  Instead of the fat of the earth;
To make such humble meals
  As honest labour can,
A bone and a crust, with a grace of God,
  And little thanks to man!

A spade! a rake! a hoe!
  A pickaxe, or a bill!
A hook to reap, or a scythe to mow,
  A flail, or what ye will—
Whatever the tool to ply,
  Here is a willing drudge,
With muscle and limb, and woe to him
  Who does their pay begrudge!

Who every weekly score
  Docks labour's little mite,
Bestows on the poor at the temple door,
  But robb'd them over night.
The very shilling he hoped to save,
  As health and morals fail,
Shall visit me in the New Bastille,
  The Spital, or the Gaol!

THOMAS HOOD

[8]

Southeast Arkanasia

After Eli Whitney's gin
brought to generations' end
bartered flesh and broken bones
Did it cleanse you of your sin
    Did you ponder?

Now, when farmers bury wheat
and the cow men dump the sweet
butter down on Davy Jones
Does it sanctify your street
      Do you wonder?

Or is guilt your nightly mare
bucking wake your evenings' share
of the stilled repair of groans
and the absence of despair
       over yonder?

MAYA ANGELOU

Song for the Old Ones

My Fathers sit on benches
        their flesh count every plank
        the slats leave dents of darkness
deep in their withered flanks.

They nod like broken candles
        all waxed and burnt profound,
        they say "It's understanding
that makes the world go round."

There in those pleated faces
        I see the auction block
        the chains and slavery's coffles
the whip and lash and stock.

My Fathers speak in voices
        that shred my fact and sound
        they say "It's our submission
that makes the world go round."

They used the finest cunning
        their naked wits and wiles
        the lowly Uncle Tomming
and Aunt Jemimas' smiles.

MAYA ANGELOU

Share-Croppers

Just a herd of Negroes
Driven to the field,
Plowing, planting, hoeing,
To make the cotton yield.

When the cotton's picked
And the work is done
Boss man takes the money
And we get none,

Leaves us hungry, ragged
As we were before.
Year by year goes by
And we are nothing more

Than a herd of Negroes
Driven to the field—
Plowing life away
To make the cotton yield.

LANGSTON HUGHES

The Closing of the Rodeo

The lariat snaps; the cowboy rolls
    His pack, and mounts and rides away.
Back to the land the cowboy goes.

Plumes of smoke from the factory sway
    In the setting sun. The curtain falls,
A train in the darkness pulls away.

Good-by, says the rain on the iron roofs.
    Good-by, say the barber poles.
Dark drum the vanishing horses' hooves.

WILLIAM JAY SMITH

Cooney Potter

I inherited forty acres from my Father
And, by working my wife, my two sons and two daughters
From dawn to dusk, I acquired
A thousand acres. But not content.
Wishing to own two thousand acres,
I bustled through the years with axe and plow,
Toiling, denying myself, my wife, my sons, my daughters.
Squire Higbee wrongs me to say
That I died from smoking Red Eagle cigars.
Eating hot pie and gulping coffee
During the scorching hours of harvest time
Brought me here ere I had reached my sixtieth year.

EDGAR LEE MASTERS

The Sower

Matt. xiii. 3

Ye sons of earth prepare the plough,
   Break up your fallow ground!
The Sower is gone forth to sow,
   And scatter blessings round.

The seed that finds a stony soil,
   Shoots forth a hasty blade;
But ill repays the sower's toil,
   Soon wither'd, scorch'd, and dead.

The thorny ground is sure to baulk
   All hopes of harvest there;
We find a tall and sickly stalk,
   But not the fruitful ear.

The beaten path and high-way side
   Receive the trust in vain;
The watchful birds the spoil divide,
   And pick up all the grain.

But where the LORD of grace and pow'r
   Has bless'd the happy field;
How plenteous is the golden store
   The deep-wrought furrows yield!

Father of mercies, we have need
   Of thy preparing grace;
Let the same hand that gives the seed,
   Provide a fruitful place!

WILLIAM COWPER

Mashkin Hill

When Levin mowed Mashkin Hill
there were moments of happy self-forgetfulness.
When he talked to a peasant who believed in God,
Levin realized that he too believed.

In the modern world there aren't any peasants.
They don't cut hay with a scythe,
or the women rake it in windrows.
Now all that work is done by machines.

Now the farmer comes home like anyone
to find that his wife has had her hair done,
and that they're dining by candlelight,
the children having been fed.

And there is no God for Levin
but the quietness of his house.

LOUIS SIMPSON

The Farm Hands

Some whirled scythes through the thick oats.
Others gathered sheaves
and made big ivory wigwams in the sun.

When they went home to rest they had dreams
of grain. The braided ears bruised their eyelids
with remembered shapes. They could not escape
the crops even in sleep.

DILYS LAING

He Was

a brown old man with a green thumb:
I can remember the screak on stones of his hoe,
The chug, choke, and high madrigal wheeze
Of the spray-cart bumping below
The sputtery leaves of the apple trees,
But he was all but dumb

Who filled some quarter of the day with sound
All of my childhood long. For all I heard
Of all his labors, I can now recall
Never a single word
Until he went in the dead of fall
To the drowsy underground,

Having planted a young orchard with so great care
In that last year that none was lost, and May
Aroused them all, the leaves saying the land's
Praise for the livening clay,
And the found voice of his buried hands
Rose in the sparrowy air.

RICHARD WILBUR

Capability Brown

Lo, he comes!
Th' omnipotent magician, Brown, appears!
Down falls the venerable pile, th' abode
Of our forefathers—a grave whisker'd race,
But tasteless. Springs a palace in its stead,
But in a distant spot; where, more expos'd,
It may enjoy th' advantage of the north,
And aguish east, till time shall have transform'd
Those naked acres to a shelt'ring grove.
He speaks. The lake in front becomes a lawn;
Woods vanish, hills subside, and vallies rise:
And streams, as if created for his use,
Pursue the track of his directing wand,
Sinuous or straight, now rapid and now slow,
Now murm'ring soft, now roaring in cascades—
Ev'n as he bids! Th' enraptur'd owner smiles.
'Tis finish'd, and yet, finish'd as it seems,
Still wants a grace, the loveliest it could show,
A mine to satisfy th' enormous cost.
Drain'd to the last poor item of his wealth,
He sighs, departs, and leaves th' accomplish'd plan
That he has touch'd, retouch'd, many a long day
Labour'd, and many a night pursu'd in dreams,
Just when it meets his hopes, and proves the heav'n
He wanted, for a wealthier to enjoy!

WILLIAM COWPER

Capability Brown. Lancelot Brown (1715–1783) was a famous English landscape gardener who assured his employers that their land held great capabilities.—H. P.

Old Florist

That hump of a man bunching chrysanthemums
Or pinching back asters, or planting azaleas,
Tamping and stamping dirt into pots,—
How he could flick and pick
Rotten leaves or yellowy petals,
Or scoop out a weed close to flourishing roots,
Or make the dust buzz with a light spray,
Or drown a bug in one spit of tobacco juice,
Or fan life into wilted sweet-peas with his hat,
Or stand all night watering roses, his feet blue in rubber boots.

THEODORE ROETHKE

An Old Charcoal Seller

An old charcoal seller
Cuts firewood, burns coal by the southern mountain.
His face, all covered with dust and ash, the color of smoke,
The hair at his temples is gray, his ten fingers black.
The money he makes selling coal, what is it for?
To put clothes on his back and food in his mouth.
The rags on his poor body are thin and threadbare;
Distressed at the low price of coal, he hopes for colder weather.
Night comes, an inch of snow has fallen on the city,
In the morning, he rides his cart along the icy ruts,
His ox weary, he hungry, and the sun already high.
In the mud by the south gate, outside the market, he stops to rest.
All of a sudden, two dashing riders appear;
An imperial envoy, garbed in yellow (his attendant in white),
Holding an official dispatch, he reads a proclamation.
Then turns the cart around, curses the ox, and leads it north.
One cartload of coal—a thousand or more catties!
No use appealing to the official spiriting the cart away:
Half a length of red lace, a slip of damask
Dropped on the ox—is payment in full!

PO CHÜ-YI
Translated from the Chinese by Eugene Eoyang

I gathered mosses in Easedale.
I saw before me,
Sitting in the open field
Upon his pack of rags,
The old Ragman that I know.
His coat is of scarlet in a thousand patches.

DOROTHY WORDSWORTH

God made the bees
And the bees make honey.
The miller's man does all the work,
But the miller makes the money.

From Mother Goose

Plowmen

A plow, they say, to plow the snow.
They cannot mean to plant it, no—
Unless in bitterness to mock
At having cultivated rock.

ROBERT FROST

At the Woodpile

Oaks are old at birth   and ornery.
Every oak holds its squatter claim
in fee.

Long before you hopefully approach—
manual in hand that tells you how
to bend an armature of branch
on which to flesh its spring with leaf,
to filter-through the sun
and custom-trim the shade—
an oak's wayward way is set.

Go prune its antlers, gorge its roots,
guy and stake—beg it heed. Still
its sap will run contrary rings
around your need, in black-tempered fury
vengeful beyond its years, whatever,
whatever time of year.

Here's an ancient hewed by winds
three winters gone—
chainsaw chewed to fire length.
There my red wedge lies where it leapt
exhausted in the snow,
spirit blunted by twisted burls:
evil sinew rusted grainless
as a matted beard.

The bleeding wedge had not once split true
before I bashed the sledge askew
and smashed its shaft.

RAYMOND HENRI

Autumn

Summer is gone and all the merry noise
Of busy harvest in its labouring glee;
The shouts of toil, the laughs of gleaning boys
Sweeing at dinner-hours on willow tree,
The cracking whip, the scraps of homely song,
Sung by the boys that drive the loaded wain,
The noise of geese that haste and hiss along
For corn that litters in the narrow lane
Torn from the wagon by the hedgerow trees,
Tinkles of whetting scythes amid the grain,
The bark of dogs stretched at their panting ease,
Watching the stook where morning's dinner lay—
All these have passed, and silence at her ease
Dreams autumn's melancholy life away.

JOHN CLARE

from Remembrances

When for school o'er Little Field with its brook and wooden brig,
Where I swaggered like a man though I was not half so big,
While I held my little plough though 'twas but a willow twig,
And drove my team along made of nothing but a name,
"Gee hep" and "hoit" and "woi"—oh, I never call to mind
These pleasant names of places but I leave a sigh behind,
While I see the little mouldiwarps hang sweeing to the wind
On the only aged willow that in all the field remains,
And nature hides her face while they're sweeing in their chains
And in a silent murmuring complains.

Here was commons for their hills, where they seek for freedom still,
Though every common's gone and though traps are set to kill
The little homeless miners—oh, it turns my bosom chill
When I think of old Sneap Green, Puddock's Nook and Hilly Snow,
Where bramble bushes grew and the daisy gemmed in dew
And the hills of silken grass like to cushions to the view,
Where we threw the pismire crumbs when we'd nothing else to do,
All levelled like a desert by the never-weary plough,
All vanished like the sun where that cloud is passing now
And settled here for ever on its brow.

Oh, I never thought that joys would run away from boys,
Or that boys would change their minds and forsake such
    summer joys;
But alack, I never dreamed that the world had other toys
To petrify first feeling like the fable into stone,
Till I found the pleasure past and a winter come at last,
Then the fields were sudden bare and the sky got overcast,
And boyhood's pleasing haunts, like a blossom in the blast,
Was shrivelled to a withered weed and trampled down and done,
Till vanished was the morning spring and set the summer sun,
And winter fought her battle strife and won.

JOHN CLARE

Iowa Land

O barn reality! I saw you swimming
clear across the cornfields of Iowa,
the loveliness and loneliness of you
deeper than the shadows of photograph.

It is a human desire! To lie down
in the damp fall on that black soil
is a human desire. To want to leave
the nuisance of the bed: its small death.

It can't just be done. We are born into
a life of avoidance, to the sun
and the tiny seeds of grains,
to the growth of the children.

A man who wakes early works in a field
Time's what he knows of the end of time
And he has something to do and what's
to die from—who's close to many, closer.

MARVIN BELL

from Boy's Will,
Joyful Labor Without Pay,
and Harvest Home (1918)

2. WORK

The hand that aches for the pitchfork heft
Heaves a sheaf from the shock's rich disrepair.
The wagoner snags it in mid-air,
Says, "Boy, save yore strength, 'fore you got none left,"
And grins, then wipes the sweat from his hair.

ROBERT PENN WARREN

Day's Work a-Done

And oh! the jaÿ our nest did yield,
  At evenèn by the mossy wall,
When we'd a-work'd all day a-vield,
  While zummer zuns did rise an' vall,
    As there a-lettèn
    Goo all frettèn,
An' vorgettèn all our twiles,
We zot among our childern's smiles.

An' under skies that glitter'd white,
  The while our smoke, arisèn blue,
Did melt in aiër, out o' zight,
  Above the trees that kept us lew;
    Wer birds a-zingèn,
    Tongues a-ringèn,
Childern springèn, vull o'jaÿ,
A-finishèn the day in plaÿ.

An' back behind, a-stannèn tall,
  The cliff did sheen to western light;
An' while avore the water-vall,
  A-rottlèn loud, an foamèn white.
    The leaves did quiver,
    Gnots did whiver,
By the river, where the pool,
In evenèn aïr did glissen cool.

An' childern there, a-runnèn wide,
  Did plaÿ their geämes along the grove
Vor though to us 'twer jaÿ to bide
  At rest, to them 'twer jaÿ to move.
    The while my smilèn
    Jeäne, beguilèn,
All my twilèn, wi' her ceäre,
Did call me to my evenèn feäre.

WILLIAM BARNES

Labours of the Months

January	By this fire I warm my hands.
February	And with my spade I delfe my lands.
March	Here I set my thynge to spring.
April	And here I hear the fowlis sing.
May	I am as light as bird in bough.
June	And I weed my corn well inow.
July	With my scythe my mead I mawe.
August	And here I shear my corn full low.
September	With my flail I earn my bread.
October	And here I sawe my wheat so red.
November	At Martinsmass I kill my swine.
December	And at Christesmass I drink red wine.

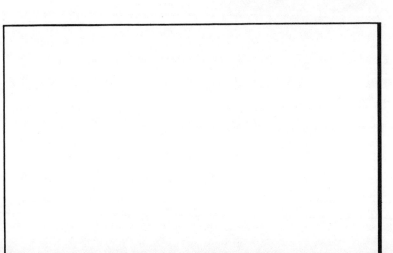

Let Her Own Work Praise Her

Proverbs XXXI: 10–31

Who can find a virtuous woman? for her price *is* far above rubies.

The heart of her husband doth safely trust in her, so that he shall have no need of spoil.

She will do him good and not evil all the days of her life.

She seeketh wool, and flax, and worketh willingly with her hands.

She is like the merchants' ships; she bringeth her food from afar.

She riseth also while it is yet night, and giveth meat to her household, and a portion to her maidens.

She considereth a field, and buyeth it: with the fruit of her hands she planteth a vineyard.

She girdeth her loins with strength, and strengtheneth her arms.

She perceiveth that her merchandise *is* good: her candle goeth not out by night.

She layeth her hands to the spindle, and her hands hold the distaff.

She stretcheth out her hand to the poor; yea, she reacheth forth her hands to the needy.

She is not afraid of the snow for her household: for all her household *are* clothed with scarlet.

She maketh herself coverings of tapestry; her clothing *is* silk and purple.

Her husband is known in the gates, when he sitteth among the elders of the land.

She maketh fine linen, and selleth *it*; and delivereth girdles unto the merchant.

Strength and honour *are* her clothing; and she shall rejoice in time to come.

She openeth her mouth with wisdom: and in her tongue *is* the law of kindness.

She looketh well to the ways of her household, and eateth not the bread of idleness.

Her children arise up, and call her blessed; her husband *also,* and
he praiseth her.
Many daughters have done virtuously, but thou excellest them all.
Favour *is* deceitful, and beauty *is* vain: *but* a woman *that* feareth
the LORD, she shall be praised.
Give her of the fruit of her hands; and let her own works praise
her in the gates.

King James Version

[36]

On St. Winefred

besides her miraculous cures
filling a bath and turning a mill

As wishing all about us sweet,
She brims her bath in cold or heat;
She lends, in aid of work and will,
Her hand from heaven to turn a mill—
Sweet soul! not scorning honest sweat
And favouring virgin freshness yet.

GERARD MANLEY HOPKINS

The Song of the Shirt

With fingers weary and worn,
   With eyelids heavy and red,
A Woman sat, in unwomanly rags,
   Plying her needle and thread—
      Stitch! stitch! stitch!
In poverty, hunger, and dirt,
      And still with a voice of dolorous pitch
She sang the "Song of the Shirt!"

"Work! work! work!
While the cock is crowing aloof!
   And work—work—work,
Till the stars shine through the roof!
It's O! to be a slave
   Along with the barbarous Turk,
Where woman has never a soul to save,
   If this is Christian work!

"Work—work—work
Till the brain begins to swim;
   Work—work—work
Till the eyes are heavy and dim!
Seam, and gusset, and band,
   Band, and gusset, and seam,
      Till over the buttons I fall asleep,
   And sew them on in a dream!

"O! Men with Sisters dear!
  O! Men! with Mothers and wives
It is not linen you're wearing out,
  But human creatures' lives!
    Stitch—stitch—stitch,
  In poverty, hunger, and dirt,
Sewing at once, with a double thread,
  A Shroud as well as a Shirt.

"But why do I talk of Death?
  That Phantom of grisly bone,
I hardly fear his terrible shape,
  It seems so like my own—
  It seems so like my own,
  Because of the fasts I keep,
Oh! God! that bread should be so dear,
  And flesh and blood so cheap!

"Work—work—work!
  My labour never flags;
And what are its wages? A bed of straw,
  A crust of bread—and rags.
That shatter'd roof,—and this naked floor—
  A table—a broken chair—
And a wall so blank, my shadow I thank
  For sometimes falling there!

"Work—work—work!
From weary chime to chime,
    Work—work—work—
As prisoners work for crime!
    Band, and gusset, and seam,
    Seam, and gusset, and band,
Till the heart is sick, and the brain benumb'd,
    As well as the weary hand.

"Work—work—work,
In the dull December light,
    And work—work—work,
When the weather is warm and bright—
While underneath the eaves
    The brooding swallows cling
As if to show me their sunny backs
    And twit me with the spring.

"Oh! but to breathe the breath
Of the cowslip and primrose sweet—
    With the sky above my head,
And the grass beneath my feet,
For only one short hour
    To feel as I used to feel,
Before I knew the woes of want
    And the walk that costs a meal!

"Oh but for one short hour!
  A respite however brief!
No blessed leisure for Love or Hope,
  But only time for Grief!
A little weeping would ease my heart,
  But in their briny bed
My tears must stop, for every drop
  Hinders needle and thread!"

[Seam, and gusset, and band,
Band, and gusset, and seam,
    Work, work, work,
Like the Engine that works by Steam!
A mere machine of iron and wood
    That toils for Mammon's sake—
Without a brain to ponder and craze
    Or a heart to feel—and break!]*

With fingers weary and worn,
  With eyelids heavy and red,
A Woman sat, in unwomanly rags,
  Plying her needle and thread—
    Stitch! stitch! stitch!
  In poverty, hunger, and dirt,
And still with a voice of dolorous pitch,
Would that its tone could reach the Rich!—
  She sang this "Song of the Shirt!"

THOMAS HOOD

*The stanza in brackets was omitted when the "Song" was originally published.

The Knitters

In companies or lone
They bend their heads, their hands
They busy with their gear,
Accomplishing the stitch
That turns the stocking-heel,
Or closes up the toe,
   These knitters at their doors.
Their talk's of nothing else
But what was told before
Sundown and gone sundown,
While goats bleat from the hill,
And men are tramping home,
   By knitters at their doors.
And we who go this way
A benediction take
From hands that ply this task
For the ten thousandth time—
   Of knitters at their doors.
Since we who deem our days
Most varied, come to own
That all the works we do
Repeat a wonted toil:
May it be done as theirs
Who turn the stocking-heel,
And close the stocking-toe,
With grace and in content,
   These knitters at their doors.

PADRAIC COLUM

Girl in a White Coat
for Penny

When there are minds to heal, and you
Among our many wounded
Like Diana move with lithe and splendid
Confidence, the local miracles come true,
    And manics whose important grief
    Threatens their lives with years of stone
Read in your eyes the excellence of life
Unfalsified by fear, untaught by pain.
Who love our lives no love will ever save
In you, my dear, may like a child believe.

    Heirs of more than we can bear,
    Our intellects must dance
On the mute graves of this inheritance.
Who may with competence receive? O who may dare
    To put his hands to the account
    Of those whose complicated gifts
We have not learned to use? Neither prophet nor saint,
Yet studied in their lore, your learning lifts
The cripple from his self-betraying stance
And shows him, in a word, his innocence.

    Our legends, as so many, say
    The measure of success
Is mere survival, yet neglect the price.
Perhaps. Perhaps. Though the atom were unlocked today
    And, razed in its explicit terror,
    Nations took their flaming signs
Into the dark, what beyond great error
Would remain? In you, my dear, I love our chance
Against the imminence of atoms; in you I love
All that our faith must find, or wisdom give.

JOHN MALCOLM BRINNIN

Looking at Quilts

Who decided what is useful in its beauty
means less than what has no function besides beauty
(except its weight in money)?
Art without frames: it held parched corn,
it covered the table where soup misted savor,
it covered the bed where the body knit
to self and other and the
dark wool of dreams

The love of the ordinary blazes out: the backyard
miracle: Ohio Sunflower,
                    Snail's Track,
                             Sweet Gum Leaf,
           Moon over the Mountain.

In the pattern Tulip and Peony the sense
of design masters the essence of what sprawled
in the afternoon: called conventionalized
to render out the intelligence, the graphic wit.

Some have a wistful faded posy yearning:
                             Star of the Four Winds,
           Star of the West,
                    Queen Charlotte's Crown.
In a crabbed humor as far from pompous
as a rolling pin, you can trace wrinkles
from smiling under a scorching grasshopper sun:

           Monkey Wrench,
                    The Drunkard's Path,
                             Fool's Puzzle,
           Puss in the Corner,
                    Robbing Peter to Pay Paul,
and the deflating
                    Hearts and Gizzards.

Pieced quilts, patchwork from best gowns,
winter woolens, linens, blankets, worked jigsaw
of the memories of braided lives, precious
scraps: women were buried but their clothing wore on.

Out of death from childbirth at sixteen, hard
work at forty, out of love for the trumpet vine
and the melon, they issue to us:
                         Rocky Road to Kansas,
          Job's Troubles,
                    Crazy Ann,
                         The Double Irish Chain,
          The Tree of Life:
                         this quilt might be
the only perfect artifact a woman
would ever see, yet she did not doubt
what we had forgotten, that out of her
potatoes and colic, sawdust and blood
she could create; together, alone,
she seized her time and made new.

MARGE PIERCY

Huswifery

Make me, O Lord, thy Spinning Wheele compleate;
 Thy Holy Worde my Distaff make for mee.
Make mine Affections thy Swift Flyers neate,
 And make my Soule thy holy Spoole to bee.
 My Conversation make to be thy Reele,
 And reele the yarn thereon spun of thy Wheele.

Make me thy Loome then, knit therein this Twine:
 And make thy Holy Spirit, Lord, winde quills:
Then weave the Web thyselfe. The yarn is fine.
 Thine Ordinances make my Fulling[1] Mills.
 Then dy the same in Heavenly Colours Choice,
 All pinkt[2] with Varnish't Flowers of Paradise.

Then cloath therewith mine Understanding, Will,
 Affections, Judgment, Conscience, Memory;
My Words and Actions, that their shine may fill
 My waves with glory and thee glorify.
 Then mine apparell shall display before yee
 That I am Cloathd in Holy robes for glory.

EDWARD TAYLOR

[1]*process of cleaning wool*
[2]*ornamented*

She sweeps with many-colored Brooms—
And leaves the Shreds behind—
Oh Housewife in the Evening West—
Come back, and dust the Pond!

You dropped a Purple Ravelling in—
You dropped an Amber thread—
And now you've littered all the East
With Duds of Emerald!

And still, she plies her spotted Brooms,
And still the Aprons fly,
Till Brooms fade softly into stars—
And then I come away—

EMILY DICKINSON

The Grandmother

Better born than married, misled,
in the heavy summers of the river bottom
and the long winters cut off by snow
she would crave gentle dainty things,
"a pretty little cookie or a cup of tea,"
but spent her days over a wood stove
cooking cornbread, kettles of jowl and beans
for the heavy, hungry, hard-handed
men she had married and mothered, bent
past unbending by her days of labor
that love had led her to. They had to break her
before she would lie down in her coffin.

WENDELL BERRY

Charwoman

(Lower Manhattan—6:00 P.M.)

Clapping the door to, in the little light,
In the stair-fall's deepening plunge,
I see, in the slate dark, the lumped form, like a sponge,
Striking a rote erasure in the night—

And keep that figure; while a watery arc
Trembles and wanes in wetted tile, as if
It wrote all darkness down in hieroglyph
And spoke vendetta with a water-mark.

That shadowy flare shall presently define
A scuffed and hazardous wrist, a ruined jaw
Packed into goitre, like a pigeon's craw,
A bitten elbow webbed with a naphtha line;

While light shall lessen, blunting, by brute degrees,
The world's waste scanted to a personal sin,
Till all is darkness where her brush has been
And blinds the blackening marble by her knees

* * *

I mark what way the dropping shaft-light went;
It flung the day's drowned faces out, and fell
Hasped like a coffin down a darkening well:

And poise on the shaft-way for my own descent.

BEN BELITT

You Owe Them Everything

Their fingers numb in thimbles,
eyes dim with hems, their front teeth gone,
they mean well. You give them old lamps.
You give them the room over the garage.
They wash your kitchen windows, looking in.
They smile like maiden aunts with lace
collars and hearing aids. They nod like doctors.
You thank them for the years on their
knees in office vestibules, the wrung-out hands,
the checks for your law books, the debts
they paid with Irish brogues in old movies.
Even your Porsche coughs in their presence.
Some of your children ask who they are
and you speak of Slavic ladies in cabbage
fields, the Haitian grandmothers dumping ashtrays.
You name the widows with varicose veins
and prominent sons who visit twice a year;
chug-a-lug maids in Hotel Edison, connoisseurs
of abandoned wine; sisters of vaudeville stars.
You hear their jangled nerves ring up in dry-
goods stores. You hear them praise children
moved to Wisconsin. They are the lost nannies
in Victorian novels, the housekeepers with rings
of keys, who put the cool cloth to hysteric
brows, who soothe like cellos in the great hall.
They know they accept everything. They know
you wake in your middle-age sweating, thinking
of them. They smoke Lucky Strikes. They buy Wonder Bread.

JOHN ALLMAN

Woman Work

I've got the children to tend
The clothes to mend
The floor to mop
The food to shop
Then the chicken to fry
The baby to dry
I got company to feed
The garden to weed
I've got the shirts to press
The tots to dress
The cane to be cut
I gotta clean up this hut
Then see about the sick
And the cotton to pick.

Shine on me, sunshine
Rain on me, rain
Fall softly, dewdrops
And cool my brow again.

Storm, blow me from here
With your fiercest wind
Let me float across the sky
'Til I can rest again.

Fall gently, snowflakes
Cover me with white
Cold icy kisses and
Let me rest tonight.

Sun, rain, curving sky
Mountain, oceans, leaf and stone
Star shine, moon glow
You're all that I can call my own.

MAYA ANGELOU

Frau Bauman, Frau Schmidt, and Frau Schwartze

Gone the three ancient ladies
Who creaked on the greenhouse ladders,
Reaching up white strings
To wind, to wind
The sweet-pea tendrils, the smilax,
Nasturtiums, the climbing
Roses, to straighten
Carnations, red
Chrysanthemums; the stiff
Stems, jointed like corn,
They tied and tucked,—
These nurses of nobody else.
Quicker than birds, they dipped
Up and sifted the dirt;
They sprinkled and shook;
They stood astride pipes,
Their skirts billowing out wide into tents,
Their hands, twinkling with wet;
Like witches they flew along rows
Keeping creation at ease;
With a tendril for needle
They sewed up the air with a stem;
They teased out the seed that the cold kept asleep,—
All the coils, loops and whorls.
They trellised the sun; they plotted for more than themselves.

I remember how they picked me up, a spindly kid,
Pinching and poking my thin ribs
Till I lay in their laps, laughing,
Weak as a whiffet;
Now, when I'm alone and cold in my bed,
They still hover over me,
These ancient leathery crones,
With their bandannas stiffened with sweat,
And their thorn-bitten wrists,
And their snuff-laden breath blowing lightly over me in
    my first sleep.

THEODORE ROETHKE

Mexical Market Woman

This ancient hag
Who sits upon the ground
Selling her scanty wares
Day in, day round,
Has known high wind-swept mountains,
And the sun has made
Her skin so brown.

LANGSTON HUGHES

Working Girls

The working girls in the morning are going to work—long lines
  of them afoot amid the downtown stores and factories,
  thousands with little brick-shaped lunches wrapped in
  newspapers under their arms.
Each morning as I move through this river of young-woman life I
  feel a wonder about where it is all going, so many with a
  peach bloom of young years on them and laughter of red lips
  and memories in their eyes of dances the night before and
  plays and walks.
Green and grey streams run side by side in a river and so here are
  always the others, those who have been over the way, the
  women who know each one the end of life's gamble for her,
  the meaning and the clue, the how and the why of the
  dances and the arms that passed around their waists and the
  fingers that played in their hair.
Faces go by written over: "I know it all, I know where the bloom
  and the laughter go and I have memories," and the feet of
  these move slower and they have wisdom where the others
  have beauty.
So the green and the grey move in the early morning on the
  downtown streets.

CARL SANDBURG

Changsha Shoe Factory

The lady director is a gentle guide. But
as Comrade Li told me

back in Hangjo, with my hands and easy
life, what can I know now

of the machine with the six old women
who smile, as all the posters

and masses smile? I am timid, even
humble, yet you are all

serene, with big watches on, as you work
the shoe and rubber belts.

The noise is a hammer but air is good,
self-reliance systems,

and I approve, and hope you approve me:
one instant like a shoe

passing down the aisle. We are not ants, and
I try to hold your face,

your tubs of hot water, the glue, and please,
remember me. Or we are lost.

WILLIS BARNSTONE

from Journal

In the evening I would sit
In my room and think of it,—
Think of fire that suddenly
Licks the wall, and none knows why,
And from the twentieth story hurls
To the pave the factory girls.

EDNA ST. VINCENT MILLAY

*On March 25, 1911, there was a fatal fire on the three top floors of the
Triangle shirtwaist factory in downtown Manhattan. More than fifty persons
were killed in the elevator shaft or after jumping from the windows. The
result of the fire was the adoption of a new building code, a review of labor
laws, and the organization of the needle trades.—H. P.*

The Little Factory Girl
to a More Fortunate Playmate

I often think how once we used in summer fields to play,
And run about and breathe the air that made us glad and gay;
We used to gather buttercups, and chase the butterfly—
I loved to feel the light breeze lift my hair as it went by!

Do you still play in those bright fields? and are the flowers still
    there?
There are no fields where I live now—no flowers any where!
But day by day I go and turn a dull and tedious wheel,
You cannot think how sad, and tired, and faint I often feel.

I hurry home to snatch the meal my mother can supply,
Then back to hasten to the task—that not to hate I try,
At night my mother kisses me, when she has combed my hair,
And laid me in my little bed, but—I'm not happy there—

I dream about the factory, the fines that on us wait—
I start and ask my father if—I have not lain too late?
And once I heard him sob and say—"Oh better were a grave,
Than such a life as this for thee, thou little sinless slave!"

I wonder if I ever shall obtain a holiday?
Oh if I do, I'll go to you, and spend it all in play.
And then I'll bring some flowers, if you will give me some;
And at my work I'll think of them and holidays to come!

The Man, May 13, 1834

*This group of poems on pages 58–65 goes back to the nineteenth century
when hundreds of young women were working in the factories of Lowell,
Massachusetts.—H. P.*

"Oh! isn't it a pity, such a pretty girl as I—
Should be sent to the factory to pine away and die?
   "Oh! I cannot be a slave,
   I will not be a slave,
   For I'm so fond of liberty
   That I cannot be a slave."

HARRIET H. ROBINSON

Ah! leave my harp and me alone
  My grief thou may'st not share,
Responsive to its plaintive tone
  Will flow refreshing tears.

Far from the factory's deaf'ning sound,
  From all its noise and strife,
Would that my years might run their rounds
  In sweep retired life.

But, if I still must wend my way,
  Uncheered by hope's sweet song,
God grant, that in the mills, a day
  May be blest, *"Ten hours"* long.

Voice of Industry, February 20, 1846

Factory Girl

No more shall I work in the factory,
Grease upon my clothes.
No more shall I work in the factory
With splinters in my toes.

No more shall I hear the metal wheels
A-rolling over my head.
When factories are hard at work,
I'll be in my bed.

No more shall I hear the whistle blow
To call me up so soon
No more shall I hear the whistle blow
To call me from my home.

No more shall I see the boss come,
All dressed up so proud.
I know I'll marry a country boy
Before the year is out.

No more shall I wear the old black dress,
Greasy all around.
No more shall I wear the old black bonnet
With holes all in the crown.

Pity me, my darling
Pity me, I say
Pity me, my darling
And carry me away.

Song from the 1870s

Song of the Factory Girls

Oh, sing me the song of the Factory Girl!
So merry and glad and free!
The bloom in her cheeks, of health how it speaks,
Oh! a happy creature is she!
She tends the loom, she watches the spindle,
And cheerfully toileth away,
Amid the din of wheels, how her bright eyes kindle,
And her bosom is ever gay.

Oh, sing me the song of the Factory Girl!
Who no titled lord doth own,
Who with treasures more rare, is more free from care
Than a queen upon her throne!
She tends the loom, she watches the spindle,
And she parts her glossy hair,
I know by her smile, as her bright eyes kindle,
That a cheerful spirit is there.

Oh, sing me the song of the Factory Girl!
Link not her name with the Slave's;
She is brave and free, as the old elm tree
Which over her homestead waves.
She tends the loom, she watches the spindle,
And scorns the laugh and the sneer,
I know by her lip, and her bright eyes kindle,
That a free born spirit is there.

Oh, sing me the song of the Factory Girl!
Whose fabric doth clothe the world,
From the king and his peers to the jolly tars
With our flag o'er all seas unfurled.
From the California's seas, to the tainted breeze
Which sweeps the smokened rooms,
Where "God save the Queen" to cry are seen
The slaves of the British looms.

Chicopee (Mass.) *Telegraph,* March 6, 1850

The Factory Girl

She wasn't the least bit pretty,
    And only the least bit gay,
And she walked with a firm, elastic tread,
    In a business kind of way;

Her dress was of coarse, brown woolen,
    Plain but neatly made,
Trimmed with some common ribbon,
    And a hat with a broken feather,
And a shawl of modest plaid.

Her face was worn and weary,
    And traced with lines of care,
As her nut brown tresses blew aside
    In the keen December air;
Yet she was not old, scarcely twenty,
    And her form was full and sleek,
But her heavy eye and tired step
    Seemed of wearisome toil to speak.
She worked as a common factory girl
    For two dollars and a half a week.

Ten hours a day of labor,
    In a close, ill-lighted room,
Machinery's buzz for music,
    Waste gas for sweet perfume;
Hot, stifling vapors in summer,
    Chill drafts on a winter's day,
No pause for rest or pleasure
    On pain of being sent away;
So ran her civilized serfdom—
FOUR CENTS an hour the pay!

"A fair day's work," say the masters,
And "a fair day's pay" say the men;
There's a strike—a raise in wages,
What effect on the poor girl then?
A harder struggle than ever
The honest path to keep,
And to sink a little lower—
Some humbler home to seek,
For rates are higher—her wages
Two dollars and a half per week.

A man gets thrice the money—
But then a "man's a man,
And a woman surely can't expect
To earn as much as he can."
Of his hire the laborer's worthy,
Be the laborer who it may;
If a woman do a man's full work,
She should have a man's full pay,
Not to be left to starve—or sin
On forty cents a day.

Two dollars and a half to live on,
Or starve on, if you will,
Two dollars and a half to dress on,
And a hungry mouth to fill;
Two dollars and a half to lodge on
In some wretched hole or den,
Where crowds are huddled together—
Girls and women and men;
If she sins to escape her bondage
Is there room for wonder then?

J. A. PHILLIPS

Machinists' Monthly Journal, September, 1895

Song of the Weaving Woman

Busy is the life of the weaving woman!
Silkworms are about to grow old after their third sleep,
And soon the silkworm goddess will start to make silk;
Early too comes this year's levy of the silk tax.
This early tax is not the evil doing of the officials—
The government has been waging wars since last year:
Soldiers in bitter fighting bandage their sword wounds;
The great general, his merits high, changes his gauze curtain.

She'd continue her effort to reel threads and weave silk,
But the tangled skeins on the loom give her trouble.

In the house to the east, a white-haired man has two daughters;
He won't marry them off because they're skilled in embroidery.
Amid the floating gossamers on the eaves,
A spider nimbly plies back and forth.
Admirable are the insects that understand Heaven's way:
They know how to spin a gossamer web in the void.

YÜAN CHEN
*Translated from the Chinese
by Wu-chi Liu*

Weaving at the Window

Sighing high and
            again a sigh!
In the garden are dates
            which the passers-by crave;
A girl of poor family
            for a rich one must weave,
Her parents beyond the wall
            can give her no help;
Cold water, rough hands,
            and fine thread so easily breaks!
Stitch in, stitch out,
            it tears at her heart!
Insects swarm in the grass,
            to cry beneath her loom,
In two days she must do
            one roll and a half;
When each tax is paid
            only odd pieces are left!
Her mother-in-law has no new dress,
            how could she wear one?
From her window she can even envy
            those green-bower girls,
Their ten fingers idle,
            while clothes fill the hamper.

WANG CHIEN
Translated from the Chinese
by William H. Nienhauser

Dawn
(As I imagine it)

The soft grey of the distant hills
Suddenly slashed with color,
Colors changing, blazing and flaming while you watch;
Colors that artists all have tried to imitate,
Tried but never quite achieved,
And through it all the sun climbs steadily over the hilltops.
Glistening grass, each dewdrop a jewel enhanced in beauty
    by the sun,
Soft summer breezes suggesting honeysuckle and new-cut hay,
The gentle lowing of cows,
The proud crowing of the rooster, as he struts about the yard,
All kinds of pleasant country noises,
Including the squeaking of the pump,
(For even that can sing a song)
And, oh, to waken with the knowledge
That all this is mine, mine for another day;
My meadows, my hay, and my cows,
My gentle, brown-eyed cows, cows that know my voice,
And glance up questioningly when I call.
A new day, a glorious day, my day!

The poems on pages 68–72 were written by young women at the
Vineyard Shore Worker's School, New York, in the 1920s.—H. P.

(As I know it)

The dawn I know is fenced by a window-frame,
Shut in by the walls of brick, high, towering walls of brick,
A patch of sky, all smudged with smoke,
No hills, no meadows, just a patch of sky,
And roofs, rows of roofs, ugly roofs,
All strung with lone lines of limp wash;
Behind these roofs somewhere the sun is rising.
This I know but have not ever seen.
No perfumed breezes here, a conglomeration of smells,
Odors of cooking breakfast mixed with the smell
Of burning rubbish in the court-yard, and noise,
The clinking of milk bottles, the rattling of dishes,
And the crying of babies, oh, so many crying babies!
The roaring of the elevated trains rushing by
That seems to reiterate—"There's no room, but you've got to
    come, you've got to come, for there is no better way!"
A new day? Yes. But city, oh cruel city!
You've killed the dawn for me!

CONSTANCE ORTMAYER

The Song of a Factory Worker

Red brick building
With many windows,
You're like a vampire,
For wherever I go,
You know
I'm coming back to you.
You have held many under your spell,
Many who have sewed
Their life away
Within your walls.
You say to me,
"Oh, you may leave
But you'll come back.
You'll miss
The whir, whir of the machinery,
The click of the tacker,
The happy laughter of the girls,
Telling jokes.
You'll miss the songs
They sing,
And the tired-eyed ones,
Watching the clock.

The pieceworkers,
Sewing fast,
So fast till it makes you dizzy
To watch.
(They haven't time to look up.)
And under the skylight,
The red-haired girl,
When the sun sets her head aflame.
You'll miss the noise and the bustle and the hurry,
And you'll come back,
You'll see."
All this and more
You say to me,
Red brick building
With many windows.

RUTH COLLINS

A Factory Rainbow

I open my eyes
And look out of the window.
It is dark.
Could it be so very early
That the sun is still hiding?
I wait a while,
Then I hear sounds,
Drops of rain on the pavements.
It is dark and gloomy,
Not pleasant to work today.
I hurry through the wet streets,
Splashing into puddles,
Crossing mud gutters.
I am greeted with a "Good morning!
A bad day to travel on!"
I am ready to work.
I look over my silk,
Dark green, deep purple, black.
Oh, what colors to run
By the sickly electric light!
I look at my color order,
I am ahead on all dark colors.
Orchid, yellow, orange and pink;
A smile passes over my face.
If I can't have the sunshine,
I can have the rainbow.

ROSE SAADI

Man may work from sun to sun
But woman's work is never done.

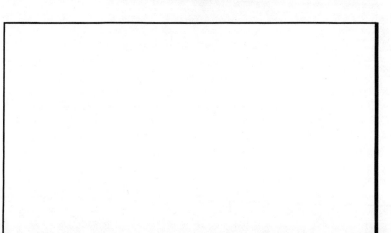

A Long Way We Come; a Long Way to Go

from Locksley Hall

Make me feel the wild pulsation that I felt before the strife,
When I heard my days before me, and the tumult of my life;

Yearning for the large excitement that the coming years would
   yield;
Eager-hearted as a boy when first he leaves his father's field,

And at night along the dusky highway near and nearer drawn,
Sees in heaven the light of London flaring like a dreary dawn;

And his spirit leaps within him to be gone before him then,
Underneath the light he looks at, in among the throngs of men;

Men, my brothers, men the workers, ever reaping something new;
That which they have done but earnest of the things that they
   shall do.

For I dipt into the future, far as human eye could see,
Saw the Vision of the world, and all the wonder that would be;

Saw the heavens fill with commerce, argosies of magic sails,
Pilots of the purple twilight, dropping down with costly bales;

Heard the heavens fill with shouting, and there rain'd a ghastly dew
From the nations' airy navies grappling in the central blue;

For along the world-wide whisper of the south-wind rushing warm,
With the standards of the peoples plunging thro' the thunder-storm;

Till the war-drum throbb'd no longer, and the battle-flags were
    furl'd
In the Parliament of man, the Federation of the world.

There the common sense of most shall hold a fretful realm in awe,
And the kindly earth shall slumber, lapt in universal law.

ALFRED, LORD TENNYSON

Boulder Dam

Not in the cities, nor among fabricated towers,
Not on the superhighways has the land been matched.
Beside the mountains, man's invention cowers.
And in a country various and wild and beautiful
How cheap the new car and the lighted movie look.
We have been hourly aware of a failure to live,
Monotonous poverty of spirit and the lack of love.

But here among hills bare and desert-red,
A violent precipice, a dizzy white curve falls
Hundreds of feet through rock to the deep canyon-bed;
A beauty sheer and clean and without error,
It stands with the created sapphire lake behind it,
It stands, a work of man as noble as the hills,
And it is faith as well as water that spills.

Not built on terror like the empty pyramid,
Not built to conquer but to illuminate a world:
It is the human answer to a human need,
Power in absolute control, freed as a gift,
A pure creative act, God when the world was born!
It proves that we have built for life and built for love
And when we are all dead, this dam will stand and give.

MAY SARTON

"You on the Tower"

I

"You on the tower of my factory—
    What do you see up there?
Do you see Enjoyment with wide wings
    Advancing to reach me here?"
—"Yea; I see Enjoyment with wide wings
    Advancing to reach you here."

II

"Good. Soon I'll come and ask you
    To tell me again thereon. . . .
Well, what is he doing now? Hoi, there!"
    —"He is still flying on."
"Ah, waiting till I have full-finished.
    Good. Tell me again anon. . . .

III

Hoi, Watchman! I'm here. When comes he?
    Between my sweats I am chill."
—"Oh, you there, working still?
Why, surely he reached you a time back,
    And took you miles from your mill?
He duly came in his winging,
    And now he has passed out of view.
How can it be that you missed him?
    He brushed you by as he flew."

THOMAS HARDY

from The True-Born Englishman

The labouring poor, in spite of double pay,
Are saucy, mutinous, and beggarly;
So lavish of their money and their time,
That want of forecast is the nation's crime.
Good drunken company is their delight;
And what they get by day they spend by night.
Dull thinking seldom does their heads engage,
But drink their youth away, and hurry on old age.
Empty of all good husbandry and sense;
And void of manners most when void of pence.
Their strong aversion to behaviour's such,
They always talk too little or too much.
So dull, they never take pains to think;
And seldom are good natured but in drink. . . .

DANIEL DEFOE

Saturday's Child

Some are teethed on a silver spoon,
  With the stars strung for a rattle;
I cut my teeth as the black raccoon—
  For implements of battle.

Some are swaddled in silk and down,
  And heralded by a star;
They swathed my limbs in a sackcloth gown
  On a night that was black as tar.

For some, godfather and goddame
  The opulent fairies be;
Dame Poverty gave me my name,
  And Pain godfathered me.

For I was born on Saturday—
  "Bad time for planting a seed,"
Was all my father had to say,
  And, "One mouth more to feed."

Death cut the strings that gave me life,
  And handed me to Sorrow,
The only kind of middle wife
  My folks could beg or borrow.

COUNTEE CULLEN

That Day

Just once
my father stopped on the way
into the house from work
and joined in the softball game
we were having in the street,
and attempted to play in *our*
game that *his* country had never
known.

Just once
and the day stands out forever
in my memory
as a father's living gesture
to his son,
that in playing even the fool
or clown, he would reveal
that the lines of their lives
were sewn from a tougher fabric
than the son had previously known.

DAVID KHERDIAN

from Peter Grimes

He built a mud-wall'd hovel, where he kept
His various wealth, and there he oft-times slept;
But no success could please his cruel soul,
He wish'd for one to trouble and control;
He wanted some obedient boy to stand
And bear the blow of his outrageous hand;
And hoped to find in some propitious hour
A feeling creature subject to his power.
   Peter had heard there were in London then,—
Still have they being!—workhouse-clearing men,
Who, undisturb'd by feelings just or kind,
Would parish-boys to needy tradesmen bind:
They in their want a trifling sum would take,
And toiling slave of piteous orphans make.
   Such Peter sought, and when a lad was found,
The sum was dealt him, and the slave was bound.
Some few in town observed in Peter's trap
A boy, with jacket blue and woollen cap;
But none inquired how Peter used the rope,
Or what the bruise, that made the stripling stoop;
None could the ridges on his back behold,
None sought him shiv'ring in the winter's cold;
None put the question,—"Peter, dost thou give
The boy his food?—What, man! the lad must live:
Consider, Peter, let the child have bread,
He'll serve thee better if he's stroked and fed."
None reason'd thus—and some,on hearing cries
Said calmly, "Grimes is at his exercise."

[84]

Pinn'd, beaten, cold, pinch'd, threaten'd, and abused—
His efforts punish'd and his food refused—
Awake tormented,—soon roused from sleep,—
Struck if he wept, and yet compell'd to weep,
The trembling boy dropp'd down and strove to pray,
Received a blow, and trembling turn'd away,
Or sobb'd and hid his piteous face;—while he,
The savage master, grinn'd in horrid glee:
He'd now the power he ever loved to show,
A feeling being subject to his blow.
    Thus lived the lad, in hunger, peril, pain,
His tears despised, his supplications vain:
Compell'd by fear to lie, by need to steal,
His bed uneasy and unbless'd his meal,
For three sad years the boy his tortures bore,
And then his pains and trials were no more.
    "How died he, Peter?" when the people said,
He growl'd—"I found him lifeless in his bed";
Then tried for softer tone, and sigh'd, "Poor Sam is dead."
Yet murmurs were there, and some questions ask'd,—
How he was fed, how punish'd, and how task'd?
Much they suspected, but they little proved,
and Peter pass'd untroubled and unmoved.

GEORGE CRABBE

The Chimney Sweeper

When my mother died I was very young,
And my father sold me while yet my tongue,
Could scarcely cry weep weep weep weep.
So your chimneys I sweep & in soot I sleep.

There's little Tom Dacre, who cried when his head
That curl'd like a lambs back, was shav'd, so I said.
Hush Tom never mind it, for when your head's bare,
You know that the soot cannot spoil your white hair.

And so he was quiet, & that very night,
As Tom was a sleeping he had such a sight,
That thousands of sweepers Dick, Joe Ned & Jack
Were all of them lock'd up in coffins of black

And by came an Angel who had a bright key,
And he open'd the coffins & set them all free.
Then down a green plain leaping laughing they run
And wash in a river and shine in the Sun.

Then naked & white, all their bags left behind,
They rise upon clouds, and sport in the wind.
And the Angel told Tom if he'd be a good boy,
He'd have God for his father & never want joy.

And so Tom awoke and we rose in the dark
And got with our bags & our brushes to work.
Tho' the morning was cold, Tom was happy & warm,
So if all do their duty, they need not fear harm.

WILLIAM BLAKE

From Songs of Innocence

The Chimney Sweeper

A little black thing among the snow:
Crying weep, weep, in notes of woe!
Where are thy father & mother? say?
They are both gone up to the church to pray.

Because I was happy upon the heath,
And smil'd among the winters snow:
They clothed me in the clothes of death,
And taught me to sing the notes of woe.

And because I am happy, & dance & sing,
They think they have done me no injury:
And are gone to Praise God & his Priest & King
Who make up a heaven of our misery.

WILLIAM BLAKE
From Songs of Experience

The Hill Above the Mine

Nobody comes to the graveyard on the hill,
sprawled on the ash-gray slope above the mine,
where coke-oven fumes drift heavily by day
and creeping fires at night. Nobody stirs
here by the crumbled wall where headstones loom
among the blackberry vines. Nobody walks
in the blue starlight under cedar branches,
twisted and black against the moon, or speaks
except the mustered company of the dead,

and one who calls the roll.
                    "Ezekiel Cowley?"
Dead.
        "Laban and Uriah Evans?"
                            Dead.
"Jasper McCullough, your three wives, your thirty
acknowledged children?"
                    Dead to the last child,
most of them buried here on the hillside, hidden
under the brambles, waiting with the others
above the unpainted cabins and the mine.

What have you seen, O dead?
                    "We saw our woods
butchered, flames curling in the maple tops,
white ashes drifting, a railroad in the valley
bridging the creek, and mine shafts under the hill.
We saw our farms lie fallow and houses grow
all summer in the flowerless meadows. Rats
all winter gnawed the last husks in the barn.
In spring the waters rose, crept through the fields
and stripped them bare of soil, while on the hill
we waited and slept firm."

                    Wait on, O dead!
The waters still shall rise, the hills fold in,
the graves open to heaven, and you shall ride
eastward on a rain wind, wrapped in thunder,
your white bones drifting like herons across the moon.

MALCOLM COWLEY

Job XXVIII:1–11

"Surely there is a mine for silver,
   and a place for gold which they refine.
Iron is taken out of the earth,
   and copper is smelted from the ore.
Men put an end to darkness,
   and search out to the farthest bound
   the ore in gloom and deep darkness.
They open shafts in a valley away from where men live;
   they are forgotten by travelers,
   they hang afar from men, they swing to and fro.
As for the earth, out of it comes bread;
   but underneath it is turned up as by fire.
Its stones are the place of sapphires,
   and it has dust of gold.

"That path no bird of prey knows,
   and the falcon's eye has not seen it.
The proud beasts have not trodden it;
   the lion has not passed over it.

"Man puts his hand to the flinty rock,
   and overturns mountains by the roots.
He cuts out channels in the rocks,
   and his eye sees every precious thing.
He binds up the streams so that they do not trickle,
   and the light that is hid he brings forth to light. . . ."

Revised Standard Version

In the coal-pit, or the factory,
 I plod by night or day;
And still, to the music o' labor
 I lilt my humble lay:
I lilt my humble lay,
 And the gloom o' the deep, deep mine,
Or the din o' the factory, dieth away,
 And a golden lot is mine.

JOSEPH SKIPSEY

The Case for the Miners

Something goes wrong with my synthetic brain
When I defend the Strikes and explain
My reasons for not blackguarding the Miners.
"What do you know?" exclaim my fellow-diners
(Peeling their plovers' eggs or lifting glasses
Of mellowed *Château Rentier* from the table),
"What do you know about the working classes?"

I strive to hold my own; but I'm unable
To state the case succinctly. Indistinctly
I mumble about World-Emancipation,
Standards of Living, Nationalization
Of Industry; until they get me tangled
In superficial details; goad me on
To unconvincing vagueness. When we've wrangled
From soup to savoury, my temper's gone.

"Why should a miner earn six pounds a week?
Leisure! They'd only spend it in a bar!
Standard of life! You'll never teach them Greek,
Or make them more contented than they are!"
That's how my port-flushed friends discuss the Strike.
And that's the reason I shout and splutter.
And that's the reason why I'd almost like
To see them hawking matches in the gutter.

SIEGFRIED SASSOON

"Butch" Weldy

After I got religion and steadied down
They gave me a job in the canning works,
And every morning I had to fill
The tank in the yard with gasoline,
That fed the blow-fires in the sheds
To heat the soldering irons.
And I mounted a rickety ladder to do it,
Carrying buckets full of the stuff.
One morning, as I stood there pouring,
The air grew still and seemed to heave,
And I shot up as the tank exploded,
And down I came with both legs broken,
And my eyes burned crisp as a couple of eggs.
For someone left a blow-fire going.
And something sucked the flame in the tank.
The Circuit Judge said whoever did it
Was a fellow-servant of mine, and so
Old Rhodes' son didn't have to pay me.
And I sat on the witness stand as blind
As Jack the Fiddler, saying over and over,
"I didn't know him at all."

EDGAR LEE MASTERS

A Lone Striker

The swinging mill bell changed its rate
To tolling like the count of fate,
And though at that the tardy ran,
One failed to make the closing gate.
There was a law of God or man
That on the one who came too late
The gate for half an hour be locked,
His time be lost, his pittance docked.
He stood rebuked and unemployed.
The straining mill began to shake.
The mill, though many-many-eyed,
Had eyes inscrutably opaque;
So that he couldn't look inside
To see if some forlorn machine
Was standing idle for his sake.
(He couldn't hope its heart would break.)

And yet he thought he saw the scene:
The air was full of dust of wool.
A thousand yarns were under pull,
But pull so slow, with such a twist,
All day from spool to lesser spool,
It seldom overtaxed their strength;
They safely grew in slender length.
And if one broke by any chance,
The spinner saw it at a glance.
The spinner still was there to spin.
That's where the human still came in.
Her deft hand showed with finger rings
Among the harplike spread of strings.
She caught the pieces end to end
And, with a touch that never missed,
Not so much tied as made them blend.
Man's ingenuity was good.
He saw it plainly where he stood,
Yet found it easy to resist.

He knew another place, a wood.
And in it, tall as trees, were cliffs;
And if he stood on one of these,
'Twould be among the tops of trees,
Their upper branches round him wreathing
Their breathing mingled with his breathing
If—if he stood! Enough of ifs!
He knew a path that wanted walking;
He knew a spring that wanted drinking;
A thought that wanted further thinking;
A love that wanted re-renewing.
Nor was this just a way of talking
To save him the expense of doing.
With him it boded action, deed.

The factory was very fine;
He wished it all the modern speed.
Yet, after all, 'twas not divine,
That is to say, 'twas not a church.
He never would assume that he'd
Be any institution's need.
But he said then and still would say,
If there should ever come a day
When industry seemed like to die
Because he left it in the lurch,

Or even merely seemed to pine
For want of his approval, why,
Come get him—they knew where to search.

ROBERT FROST

An Ode to the Framers of the Frame Bill

Oh well done Lord E—n! and better done R—r!
  Britannia must prosper with councils like yours;
Hawkesbury, Harrowby, help you to guide her,
  Whose remedy only must kill ere it cures:
Those villains, the Weavers, are all grown refractory,
  Asking some succour for Charity's sake—
So hang them in clusters round each Manufactory,
  That will at once put an end to *mistake*.

The rascals, perhaps, may betake them to robbing,
  The dogs to be sure have got nothing to eat—
So if we can hang them for breaking a bobbin,
  'T will save all the Government's money and meat:
Men are more easily made than machinery—
  Stockings fetch better prices than lives—
Gibbets on Sherwood will heighten the scenery,
  Shewing how Commerce on Liberty thrives!

Justice is now in pursuit of the wretches,
  Grenadiers, Volunteers, Bow-street Police,
Twenty-two Regiments, a score of Jack Ketches,
  Three of the Quorum and two of the Peace;
Some Lords, to be sure, would have summon'd the Judges,
  To take their opinion, but that they ne'er shall,
For LIVERPOOL such a concession begrudges.
  So now they're condemn'd by *no Judges* at all.

[96]

Some folks for certain have thought it was shocking,
  When Famine appeals and when Poverty groans,
That life should be valued at less than a stocking,
  And breaking of frames lead to breaking of bones.
If it should prove so, I trust, by this token
  (And who will refuse to partake in the hope?),
That the frames of the fools may be first to be *broken*,
  Who, when asked for a *remedy*, sent them a *rope*.

GEORGE GORDON, LORD BYRON

*Byron wrote this poem in 1812 in defence of the Luddites who, from 1811 to
1816, broke machines in protest against unemployment. Ned Lud, the
leader who broke two stocking frames, was called General Lud.—H. P.*

Song
To the Men of England

I
Men of England, wherefore plough
For the lords who lay ye low?
Wherefore weave with toil and care
The rich robes your tyrants wear?

II
Wherefore feed, and clothe, and save,
From the cradle to the grave,
Those ungrateful drones who would
Drain your sweat—nay, drink your blood?

III
Wherefore, Bees of England, forge
Many a weapon, chain, and scourge,
That these stingless drones may spoil
The forced produce of your toil?

IV
Have ye leisure, comfort, calm,
Shelter, food, love's gentle balm?
Or what is it ye buy so dear
With your pain and with your fear?

V
The seed ye sow, another reaps;
The wealth ye find, another keeps;
The robes ye weave, another wears;
The arms ye forge, another bears.

VI

Sow seed,—but let no tyrant reap;
End wealth,—let no impostor heap;
Weave robes,—let not the idle wear;
Forge arms,—in your defence to bear.

VII

Shrink to your cellars, holes, and cells;
In halls ye deck, another dwells.
Why shake the chains ye wrought? Ye see
The steel ye tempered glance on ye.

VIII

With plough and spade, and hoe and loom,
Trace your grave, and build your tomb,
And weave your winding-sheet, till fair
England be your sepulchre.

PERCY BYSSHE SHELLEY

This poem is to be ascribed to Shelley's renewed political excitement owing
to the Manchester Massacre, usually known as Peterloo. It took place in
August, 1819, when a crowd gathered at St. Peters Field to petition
Parliament for redress of grievances. The Riot Act was read in such a way
that it was not heard by most of the people. Panic ensued and the soldiers
were ordered to fire on the crowd. Several of the petitioners were killed and
many more injured, and indignation was aroused throughout England.—H. P.

The Four Dears

Dear Sugar, dear Tea, and dear Corn
  Conspired with dear Representation,
To laugh worth and honour to scorn,
  And beggar the whole British nation.

Let us bribe the dear sharks, said dear Tea;
  Bribe, bribe, said dear Representation;
Then buy with their own the dear humbugg'd and be
  The bulwarks of Tory dictation.

Dear Sugar and Tea, said dear Corn,
  Be true to dear Representation;
And then the dear crown will be worn,
  But to dignify dearest taxation.

Dear Sugar, dear Corn, and dear Tea,
  Stick to me, said dear Representation;
Let us still pull together, and we
  Shall still rob the dear British nation.

EBENEZER ELLIOTT

*Ebenezer Elliott made a passionate attack on the Corn Laws which raised
the cost of living in England so high that many of the poor faced
starvation. Corn Law Rhymes, from which these two poems come,
appeared in 1833.—H. P.*

Song

Tune—"Robin Adair."

Child, is thy father dead?
  Father is gone!
Why did they tax his bread?
  God's will be done!
Mother has sold her bed;
Better to die than wed!
Where shall she lay her head?
  Home we have none!

Father clamm'd thrice a week,
  God's will be done!
Long for work did he seek,
  Work he found none.
Tears on his hollow cheek
Told what no tongue could speak:
Why did his master break?
  God's will be done!

Doctor said air was best,
  Food we had none;
Father, with panting breast,
  Groan'd to be gone:
Now he is with the blest—
Mother says death is best!
We have no place of rest—
  Yes, ye have one!

EBENEZER ELLIOTT

Driving at Dawn

Driving at dawn past Buffalo
we point to steel mills' stacks
reddening the sky as though
they threaten to set it afire. Hereabouts
soot rains steadily on the shacks
of steelmen and their ashen wives,
once sparks themselves in other lives
that burned a while, but then went out.

A limbo of gray trees and grass, then
a few miles more
and roadsides are green again
under the sun. This arsonist,
rising with matches in his fist,
glaring our windshield's ash on fire,
burns again for the steelmen
who burned like hell for their women.

WILLIAM HEYEN

The Gnomes

Poring over a book, or my sewing,
eyes narrowed and often, now
failing to see exactly,
I am my grandfather tailoring twin

coats for his dark-haired daughters, Semitic
eyes measuring thick stuff as
he cuts and stitches: innocent
as the eyes of the boy-apprentice in

Odessa, who, looking out at the white
streets, laughed at the snow; St. Paul
is not much different. Later
I see him staring up from his desk at

his store, owlish with reading, spectacled;
there are piles of papers; he
imagines stories and his
ill-formed letters slowly construct a house.

I breathe in miasmas of shoe-boxes
filled with stiff leather, rubber
boots, blue denim overalls:
ancient unturned merchandise. He is a

small gnome in that cave of commodity,
yellow-skinned and bald, fingers
gnarled and long as pencils; and
he is desirous of solitude. As

he turns, our eyes merge in myopic vision.
We walk together into
that murky cavern, peering
near-sightedly down its furthest reaches.

BETH BENTLEY

Willis Beggs

Did I reach the pinnacle of success,
Friends of Spoon River?
Did thrift, industry, courage, honesty
Used for the increase of the canning works
Become other than thrift, industry, courage, honesty
As applied to the canning works?
Are the mechanics of civilization
Civilization itself?
Or are they tools with which factories may be built,
Or Parthenons?
I fashioned my own prison, friends of Spoon River;
I put walls between myself and a full life,
Between myself and happiness,
Except the happiness of work.
And all the while I could look out of a window
Upon an America perishing for life,
Never to be attained
By thrift, industry and courage
Dedicated to the canning works!

EDGAR LEE MASTERS

The Boss

Skilled to pull wires, he baffles Nature's hope,
Who sure intended him to stretch a rope.

JAMES RUSSELL LOWELL

Muckers

Twenty men stand watching the muckers.
Stabbing the sides of the ditch
Where clay gleams yellow,
Driving the blades of their shovels
Deeper and deeper for the new gas mains,
Wiping sweat off their faces
          With red bandannas.
The muckers work on . . . pausing . . . to pull
Their boots out of suckholes, where they slosh.

    Of the twenty looking on
Ten murmur, "Oh, it's a hell of a job,"
Ten others, "Jesus, I wish I had the job."

CARL SANDBURG

Brother, Can You Spare a Dime?

They used to tell me I was building a dream
And so I followed the mob.
When there was earth to plough or guns to bear
I was always there—right on the job.
They used to tell me I was building a dream
With peace and glory ahead,
Why should I be standing in line just waiting for bread?
Once I built a railroad, made it run,
Made it race against time.
Once I built a railroad, Now it's done—
Brother, can you spare a dime?
Once I built a tower, to the sun—
Brick and rivet and lime,
Once I built a tower, Now it's done,
Brother, can you spare a dime?
Once in khaki suits, Gee, we looked swell,
Full of that Yankee-Doodle-de-dum.
Half a million boots went sloggin' thru Hell,
I was the kid with the drum.
Say, don't you remember, they called me Al
It was Al all the time.
Say, don't you remember I'm your Pal!
Buddy, can you spare a dime?

E. Y. HARBURG

He said he had been a soldier,
That his wife and children
Had died in Jamaica.
He had a beggar's wallet over his shoulders,
And a coat of shreds and patches.
And though his body was bent,
He was tall
And had the look of one
Used to have been upright.

I talked a while, and then
I gave him a piece of cold bacon
And a penny.

DOROTHY WORDSWORTH

Vagabonds

We are the desperate
Who do not care,
The hungry
Who have nowhere
To eat,
No place to sleep,
The tearless
Who cannot
Weep.

LANGSTON HUGHES

Tiempo Muerto

Batata and rice
or rice alone
or fish if there was fish
sweet potato and fish

Nothing shook my grandmother's house
Water that ran in the river
left the banks unchanged

Lloréns Torres to New York
came in July looking for snowflakes
Trained as a welder in Newark
no welders wanted
Tobacco in Hartford
Apples on Route 202
Vagrant in Greenfield
winter in Springfield
food stamps in Boston

Batata and rice
or rice alone
or fish if there was fish
sweet potato and fish

Run
grandmother
run
River's in flood
animals bloated and drowned

The late noon high
comes and goes
Beer is still cheaper
than wine
Found no work
spent the day
burning gasoline

RICARDO ALONSO

Tiempo Muerto, *"dead time."* *The five months of the year that canecutters*
spent unemployed.
Lloréns Torres, *housing project in San Juan, Puerto Rico.*

Trinity Place

The pigeons that peck at the grass in Trinity Churchyard
   Are pompous as bankers. They walk with an air, they preen
Their prosperous feathers. They smugly regard their beauty.
They are plump, they are sleek. It is only the men who are lean.
The pigeons scan with disfavor the men who sit there,
   Listless in sun or shade. The pigeons sidle
Between the gravestones with shrewd, industrious motions.
   The pigeons are busy. It is only the men who are idle.
The pigeons sharpen their beaks on the stones, and they waddle
   In dignified search of their proper, their daily bread.
Their eyes are small with contempt for the men on the benches.
   It is only the men who are hungry. The pigeons are fed.

PHYLLIS McGINLEY

Blacklisted

Why shall I keep the old name?
What is a name anywhere anyway?
A name is a cheap thing all fathers and mothers leave each child:
A job is a job and I want to live, so
Why does God Almighty or anybody else care whether I take a
    new name to go by?

CARL SANDBURG

from "Halleluyah I'm a Bum"

Oh why don't you work
Like other men do?
How the hell can I work
When there's no work to do?

Around 1907

I've Been Workin' on the Railroad

I've been workin' on the railroad
All the livelong day.
I've been workin' on the railroad
Just to pass the time away.
Don't you hear the whistle blowing?
Rise up so early in the morn.
Don't you hear the Captain shouting:
"Dinah, blow your horn."

Toads Revisited

Walking around in the park
Should feel better than work:
The lake, the sunshine,
The grass to lie on,

Blurred playground noises
Beyond black-stockinged nurses—
Not a bad place to be.
Yet it doesn't suit me,

Being one of the men
You meet of an afternoon:
Palsied old step-takers,
Hare-eyed clerks with the jitters,

Waxed-fleshed out-patients
Still vague from accidents,
And characters in long coats
Deep in the litter-baskets—

All dodging the toad work
By being stupid or weak.
Think of being them!
Hearing the hours chime,

Watching the bread delivered,
The sun by clouds covered,
The children going home;
Think of being them,

Turning over their failures
By some bed of lobelias,
Nowhere to go but indoors,
No friends but empty chairs—

No, give me my in-tray,
My loaf-haired secretary,
My shall-I-keep-the-call-in-Sir:
What else can I answer,

When the lights come on at four
At the end of another year?
Give me your arm, old toad;
Help me down Cemetery Road.

PHILIP LARKIN

Men Working

Charming, the movement of girls about a May-pole in May,
Weaving the coloured ribbons in and out,
Charming; youth is charming, youth is fair.

But beautiful the movement of men striking pikes
Into the end of a black pole, and slowly
Raising it out of the damp grass and up into the air.
The clean strike of the pike into the pole: beautiful.

Joe is the boss; but Ed or Bill will say,
"No, Joe; we can't get it that way—
We've got to take it from here. Are you okay
On your side, Joe?" "Yes," says the boss. "Okay."

The clean strike of the pike into the pole—*"That's it!"*
"Ground your pikes!"

The grounded pikes about the rising black pole, beautiful.
"Ed, you'd better get under here with me!" "I'm
Under!"
"That's it!"
"Ground your pikes!"

Joe says, "Now, boys, don't heave
Too hard—we've got her—but you, Ed, you and Mike,
You'll have to hold her from underneath while Bill
Shifts his pike—she wants to fall downhill;
We've got her all right, but we've got her on a slight
Slant."
"That's it!"—"Mike,
About six feet lower this time."
"That's it!"

"Ground your pikes!"

One by one the pikes are moved about the pole, more beautiful
Than coloured ribbons weaving.

The clean strike of the pike into the pole; each man
Depending on the skill
And the balance, both of body and of mind,
Of each of the others: in the back of each man's mind
The respect for the pole: it is forty feet high, and weighs
Two thousand pounds.

In the front of each man's mind: "She's going to go
Exactly where we want her to go: this pole
Is going to go into that seven-foot hole we dug
For her
To stand in."

This was in the deepening dusk of a July night.
They were putting in the poles: bringing the electric light.

EDNA ST. VINCENT MILLAY

Work Gangs

Box cars run by a mile long.
And I wonder what they say to each other
When they stop a mile long on a sidetrack.
          Maybe their chatter goes:
I came from Fargo with a load of wheat up to the danger line.
I came from Omaha with a load of shorthorns and they splintered
          my boards.
I came from Detroit heavy with a load of flivvers.
I carried apples from the Hood river last year and this year
          bunches of bananas from Florida; they look for me with
          watermelons from Mississippi next year.

Hammers and shovels of work gangs sleep in shop corners
when the dark stars come on the sky and the night watchmen
          walk and look.

Then the hammer heads talk to the handles,
then the scoops of the shovels talk,
how the day's work nicked and trimmed them,
how they swung and lifted all day,
how the hands of the work gangs smelled of hope.
In the night of the dark stars
when the curve of the sky is a work gang handle,
in the night on the mile-long sidetracks,
in the night where the hammers and shovels sleep in corners,
the night watchmen stuff their pipes with dreams—
and sometimes they doze and don't care for nothin',
and sometimes they search their heads for meanings, stories, stars.

The stuff of it runs like this:
A long way we come; a long way to go; long rests and long deep
    sniffs for our lungs on the way.
Sleep is a belonging of all; even if all songs are old songs and the
    singing heart is snuffed out like a switchman's lantern with the
    oil gone, even if we forget our names and houses in the
    finish, the secret of sleep is left us, sleep belongs to all, sleep
    is the first and last and best of all.

People singing; people with song mouths connecting with song
    hearts; people who must sing or die; people whose song
    hearts break if there is no song mouth; these are my people.

CARL SANDBURG

Telephone Poles

They have been with us a long time.
They will outlast the elms.
Our eyes, like the eyes of a savage sieving the trees
In his search for game,
Run through them. They blend along small-town streets
Like a race of giants that have faded into mere mythology.
Our eyes, washed clean of belief,
Lift incredulous to their fearsome crowns of bolts, trusses, struts,
      nuts, insulators, and such
Barnacles as compose
These weathered encrustations of electrical debris—
Each a Gorgon's head, which, seized right,
Could stun us to stone.

Yet they are ours. We made them.
See here, where the cleats of linemen
Have roughened a second bark
Onto the bald trunk. And these spikes
Have been driven sideways at intervals handy for human legs.
The Nature of our construction is in every way
A better fit than the Nature it displaces.
What other tree can you climb where the birds' twitter,
Unscrambled, is English? True, their thin shade is negligible,
But then again there is not that tragic autumnal
Casting-off of leaves to outface annually.
These giants are more constant than evergreens
By being never green.

JOHN UPDIKE

Nightmare Number Three

We had expected everything but revolt
And I kind of wonder myself when they started thinking—
But there's no dice in that now.
                    I've heard fellows say
They must have planned it for years and maybe they did.
Looking back, you can find little incidents here and there,
Like the concrete-mixer in Jersey eating the wop
Or the roto press that printed "Fiddle-dee-dee!"
In a three-color process all over Senator Sloop,
Just as he was making a speech. The thing about that
Was, how could it walk upstairs? But it was upstairs,
Clicking and mumbling in the Senate Chamber.
They had to knock out the wall to take it away
And the wrecking-crew said it grinned.
                    It was only the best
Machines, of course, the superhuman machines,
The ones we'd built to be better than flesh and bone,
But the cars were in it, of course . . .
                    and they hunted us
Like rabbits through the cramped streets on that Bloody Monday,
The Madison Avenue busses leading the charge.
The busses were pretty bad—but I'll not forget
The smash of glass when the Duesenberg left the show-room
And pinned three brokers to the Racquet Club steps
Or the long howl of the horns when they saw men run,
When they saw them looking for holes in the solid ground . . .
I guess they were tired of being ridden in
And stopped and started by pygmies for silly ends,
Of wrapping cheap cigarettes and bad chocolate bars
Collecting nickels and waving platinum hair
And letting six million people live in a town.
I guess it was that. I guess they got tired of us
And the whole smell of human hands.

                                        But it was a shock
To climb sixteen flights of stairs to Art Zuckow's office
(Nobody took the elevators twice)
And find him strangled to death in a nest of telephones,
The octopus-tendrils waving over his head,
And a sort of quiet humming filling the air. . . .
Do they eat? . . . There was red . . . But I did not stop to look.
I don't know yet how I got to the roof in time
And it's lonely, here on the roof.
                                For a while, I thought
That window-cleaner would make it, and keep me company.
But they got him with his own hoist at the sixteenth floor
And dragged him in, with a squeal.
You see, they coöperate. Well, we taught them that
And it's fair enough, I suppose. You see, we built them.
We taught them to think for themselves.
It was bound to come. You can see it was bound to come.
And it won't be so bad, in the country. I hate to think
Of the reapers, running wild in the Kansas fields,
And the transport planes like hawks on a chickenyard,
But the horses might help. We might make a deal with the horses.
At least, you've more chance, out there.
                                And they need us, too.
They're bound to realize that when they once calm down.
They'll need oil and spare parts and adjustments and tuning up.
Slaves? Well, in a way, you know, we were slaves before.
There won't be so much real difference—honest, there won't.
(I wish I hadn't looked into that beauty-parlor
And seen what was happening there.
But those are female machines and a bit high-strung.)
Oh, we'll settle down. We'll arrange it. We'll compromise.
It wouldn't make sense to wipe out the whole human race.
Why, I bet if I went to my old Plymouth now
(Of course you'd have to do it the tactful way.)
And said, "Look here! Who got you the swell French horn?"
He wouldn't turn me over to those police cars;
At least I don't think he would.

Oh, it's going to be jake.
There won't be so much real difference—honest, there won't—
And I'd go down in a minute and take my chance—
I'm a good American and I always liked them—
Except for one small detail that bothers me
And that's the food proposition. Because, you see,
The concrete-mixer may have made a mistake,
And it looks like just high spirits.
But, if it's got so they like the flavor . . . well . . .

STEPHEN VINCENT BENÉT

What a Prodigious Step to Have Taken

I Hear America Singing

I hear America singing, the varied carols I hear,
Those of mechanics, each one singing his as it should be blithe
and strong,
The carpenter singing his as he measures his plank or beam,
The mason singing his as he makes ready for work, or leaves off
work,
The boatman singing what belongs to him in his boat, the deck-
hand singing on the steamboat deck,
The shoemaker singing as he sits on his bench, the hatter singing
as he stands,
The wood-cutter's song, the ploughboy's on his way in the
morning, or at noon intermission or at sundown,
The delicious singing of the mother, or of the young wife at work,
or of the girl sewing or washing,
Each singing what belongs to him or her and to none else,
The day what belongs to the day—at night the party of young
fellows, robust, friendly,
Singing with open mouths their strong melodious songs.

WALT WHITMAN

With a Posthumous Medal

His hands were talented for intricate transactions;
He might, but for the time, have planned a city
Or written music all night in splendid rooms
Or righted recalcitrant hollyhocks or children;
He might have died after a wide and easy fame
As a farmer does, or a cutter of stones.

But in the astonishment of midnight, the lewd transactions
Of hunger and homelessness, where all are children,
He could not know his eyes had turned to stones;
On the river margins of a stricken city
He survived his childhood in unpainted rooms
With a criminal's stance and a movie's idea of fame.

In the disputations on gardens or locker-rooms
He might, but for the time, be leader of transactions
In a white suburb, or mayor of a city
Fretfully occupied with laying cornerstones.
Aesthetics of mere living might have won him fame
In the staunch songs of his children's children.

But the time was all against him in the impoverished city;
While fathers asked for bread and broke their teeth on stones
And comic pictures fed hungry children,
The future was walled in a director's room
By the men from Radio City, where fame
Like death stalks market-page transactions.

He might have been whole and honored in his city
For having assured the straightness of its children;
He might have known the individuality and fame
Of the human nemesis of cancer. On public stones
His people might have read genius and the transactions
Of genius, and told of it throughout their common rooms.

[130]

But in the lists of soldiery, by official transactions,
His name was a number and he had no fame;
When he left his unlived life, and the rooms
Where nothing is wholly alive, though the children
Still duelled to the death with their sticks and stones,
There was law and order all over the city.

How little his poverty had to do with his fame
One day, when, far from dispirited rooms,
He fell, not even in flames, toward another city.
The objective was successful in the book of transactions,
Though this was but a death among ruined stones
Of one who knew them with the intimacy of children.

JOHN MALCOLM BRINNIN

The Fishvendor

Where he stood in boots in water to his calves,
A kind of fisherman, dispensing with a dip-net
Sullen carp into the tubs of ice,
Was only in a tank on the back of a truck.
Blocks off, gulls rung and fell to investigate
What they took to be sardine cans
On the river shiningly; but who contended
For his thick brown fish were rather wives
With boiling dishes in their eyes,
Women estranged by city from live water;
Where even the cats did not wait for the heads,
The scene was that strong.

While the mistaken sea-birds thrust the city away
With a salt vigor,
I heard the fisherman's feet shift in the brine,
The thick fish thrashing without resignation,
The shoppers, half tame at noon,
Naming the coins that routed all of the cats
And were for salt and instinct to a city.

WILLIAM MEREDITH

Le Médecin Malgré Lui

Oh I suppose I should
wash the walls of my office
polish the rust from
my instruments and keep them
definitely in order
build shelves in the laboratory
empty out the old stains
clean the bottles
and refill them, buy
another lens, put
my journals on edge instead of
letting them lie flat
in heaps—then begin
ten years back and
gradually
read them to date
cataloguing important
articles for ready reference.
I suppose I should
read the new books.
If to this I added
a bill at the tailor's
and at the cleaner's
grew a decent beard
and cultivated a look
of importance—
Who can tell? I might be
a credit to my Lady Happiness
and never think anything
but a white thought!

WILLIAM CARLOS WILLIAMS

Epitaph on an Army of Mercenaries

These, in the day when heaven was falling,
　The hour when earth's foundations fled,
Followed their mercenary calling
　And took their wages and are dead.

Their shoulders held the sky suspended;
　They stood, and earth's foundations stay;
What God abandoned, these defended,
　And saved the sum of things for pay.

A. E. HOUSMAN

Mendings

for Alfred Marshak

You made healing as you wanted us to make bread and poems.
In your abrasive life of gifts,
In the little ravine the life of the future
When your science would be given to all,
A broken smile.
In the sun, speaking of the joining of nerve-endings,
Make the wounds part of the well body.
Make a healed life.
You shouted, waving your hand with the last phalange
Of the little finger missing, you whole man,
"Make it well! Make things accessible!"
He is a pollinating man. We are his seedlings.
Marshak, I was your broken nerve-endings,
You made your man-made bridges over the broken nerves.
What did you do? Inspect potatoes, wait for passports, do your
    research,
While the State Department lady was saying, "Let him swim,"
While the chief who had the power to allow your uses
To move, a proper use of plastic, a bridge across broken nerves
Stopped you there (and asked me to marry him).
Saying to you, Marshak, full of creation as the time
Went deeper into war, and you to death:
"The war will be over before your work is ready."

MURIEL RUKEYSER

John Grumlie

John Grumlie swore by the light o' the moon
    And the green leaf on the tree
That he could dae more wark in a day
    Than his wife could dae in three.

*On the University Carrier who sickn'd in
the time of his vacancy, being forbid
to go to* London *by reason of the* Plague

Here lies old *Hobson,* Death hath broke his girt,
And here alas, hath laid him in the dirt,
Or els the ways being foul, twenty to one,
He's here stuck in a slough, and overthrown.
'Twas such a shifter, that if truth were known,
Death was half glad when he had got him down;
For he had any time this ten yeers full,
Dodg'd with him, betwixt *Cambridge* and the Bull.
And surely, Death could never have prevail'd,
Had not his weekly course of carriage fail'd;
But lately finding him so long at home,
And thinking now his journeys end was come,
And that he had tane up his latest Inne,
In the kind office of a Chamberlin
Shew'd him his room where he must lodge that night,
Pull'd off his Boots, and took away the light:
If any ask for him, it shall be sed,
Hobson has supt, and's newly gone to bed.

JOHN MILTON

*Thomas Hobson was a liveryman in Cambridge, England, who obliged his
customers to "take the horse which stood near the stable door" (Steele,*
Spectator #509). *Hence the expression "Hobson's choice," which means
this or none.—H. P.*

Prayer Before Work

Great one, austere,
By whose intent the distant star
Holds its course clear,
Now make this spirit soar—
Give it that ease.

Out of the absolute
Abstracted grief, comfortless, mute,
Sound the clear note,
Pure, piercing as the flute:
Give it precision.

Austere, great one,
By whose grace the inalterable song
May still be wrested from
The corrupt lung:
Give it strict form.

MAY SARTON

from Reverdure

One thing work gives
is the joy of not working,
a minute here or there
when I stand and only breathe,
receiving the good of the air.
It comes back. Good work done
comes back into the mind,
a free breath drawn.

WENDELL BERRY

Work Without Hope

All Nature seems at work. Slugs leave their lair—
The bees are stirring—birds are on the wing—
And Winter slumbering in the open air,
Wears on his smiling face a dream of Spring!
And I, the while, the sole unbusy thing,
Nor honey make, nor pair, nor build, nor sing.

Yet well I ken the banks where Amaranths blow,
Have traced the fount whence streams of nectar flow.
Bloom, O ye Amaranths! bloom for whom ye may,
For me ye bloom not! Glide, rich streams, away!
With lips unbrightened, wreathless brow, I stroll:
And would you learn the spells that drowse my soul?
Work without Hope draws nectar in a sieve,
And Hope without an object cannot live.

SAMUEL TAYLOR COLERIDGE

My Jacket Old

My jacket old, with narrow seam—
When the dull day's work is done
I dust it, and of Asia dream,
Old Asia of the sun!
There other garbs prevail;
Yea, lingering there, free robe and vest
Edenic Leisure's age attest
Ere Work, alack, came in with Wail.

HERMAN MELVILLE

Work, for the night is coming;
   Work through the morning hours;
Work, while the dew is sparkling;
   Work, 'mid springing flowers:
Work, when the day grows brighter,
   Work, in the glowing sun;
Work, for the night is coming,
   When man's work is done.

Work, for the night is coming;
   Work through the sunny noon,
Fill brightest hours with labor;
   Rest comes sure and soon.
Give every flying minute
   Something to keep in store;
Work, for the night is coming,
   When man works no more.

Work, for the night is coming,
   Under the sunset skies;
While their bright tints are glowing,
   Work, for daylight flies.
Work, till the last beam fadeth,
   Fadeth to shine no more:
Work, while the night is dark'ning,
   When man's work is o'er.

ANNIE L. WALKER

[142]

Dislike of Tasks

In sour seasons, in diff-
icult wind, stubborn snow,
handle the stiff
work, resistant thought, know

weight harder than force
hurting hands, the black
idea of failure. Your course
is one forward, two back.

Frozen, can't unlock it.
Sticks in the socket.

Material not made
for such use
fights needle and blade,
resists, or works loose.

In sour seasons, pursue
the impossible task, the year's
new repulse. All true
silk purses are made of sows' ears.
It's hard to do.

RICHMOND LATTIMORE

The Outwit Song

My only desire was to make myself over
In a poem's truth and delight.
Then the life that I lived became Work-of-the-World
And banished joy from sight.
>*But I can outwit him.*

I wheeled as a bird with an acrobat's wing
And a throat like an angel's oboe.
He turned into spray that poisons the seed
On the weed where the finches sing as they feed,
>*But I can outwit him.*

I made myself be a great beech tree,
All green at the head and the mantle green.
Then just where my shade fell in a cool glade
He bulldozed a hot level parking lot,
>*But I can outwit him.*

I swiftly became a seam of coal,
A million years compressed in my soul.
With eminent domain and shovel and train
He gouged the hill so I'd burn in a mill,
>*But I can outwit him.*

I was the wind that can sigh and sing
And make the world a harp at my will,
He was the ash and the acrid trash
Of the city that chokes on its swill.
        But I can outwit him.

I'll remake my shape as a coil of punched tape,
A drudge among drudges that toil.
He'll turn into a new computer.
He'll gobble me whole and print out my soul,
        But I can outwit him.

I'll program him to say that I most want to be
The joy and truth of a poem.
He will turn into dull Work-of-the-World
Unmoved by the sight of another's delight,
        But I can outwit him.

DANIEL HOFFMAN

Talk with a Poet

A thing Dylan Thomas once said
About poetry haunts me most—
Still echoed derisively
By his sweating, chainsmoking ghost,
Told me in anger first
By the public poet who read
His verse on platforms aloud:
"Fool," the poems said,
"Why don't you go back to work?"

Spoken in mocking rage
Of words, words he did not write,
All the shining handiwork
Half-wrought in that good night,
All the images of the dream
Too quickly forfeited—
I hear his dark voice again:
"Fool!" the poems said,
Scornfully. But he is dead.

HELEN BEVINGTON

Application for a Grant

Noble executors of the munificent testament
Of the late John Simon Guggenheim, distinguished bunch
Of benefactors, there are certain kinds of men
Who set their hearts on being bartenders,
For whom a life upon duck-boards, among fifths,
Tapped kegs and lemon twists, crowded with lushes
Who can master neither their bladders nor consonants,
Is the only life, greatly to be desired.
There's the man who yearns for the White House, there to compose
Rhythmical lists of enemies, while someone else
Wants to be known to the *Tour d'Argent's* head waiter.
As the Sibyl of Cumae said: It takes all kinds.
Nothing could bribe your Timon, your charter member
Of the Fraternal Order of Grizzly Bears to love
His fellow, whereas it's just the opposite
With interior decorators; that's what makes horse races.
One man may have a sharp nose for tax shelters,
Screwing the IRS with mirth and profit;
Another devote himself to his shell collection,
Deaf to his offspring, indifferent to the feast
With which his wife hopes to attract his notice.
Some at the Health Club sweating under bar bells
Labor away like grunting troglodytes,
Smelly and thick and inarticulate,
Their brains squeezed out through their pores by sheer exertion.
As for me, the prize for poets, the simple gift
For amphybrachs strewn by a kind Euterpe,
With perhaps a laurel crown of the evergreen
Imperishable of your fine endowment
Would supply my modest wants, who dream of nothing
But a pad on Eighth Street and your approbation.

(Freely from Horace)

ANTHONY HECHT

Horace, Odes, Book I, Ode 1

Junk

Huru Welandes
      worc ne geswiceð
monna ænigum
      ðara ðe Mimming can
heardne gehealdan.
        WALDERE

An axe angles
      from my neighbor's ashcan;
It is hell's handiwork,
      the wood not hickory,
The flow of the grain
      not faithfully followed.
The shivered shaft
      rises from a shellheap
Of plastic playthings,
      paper plates,
And the sheer shards
      of shattered tumblers
That were not annealed
      for the time needful.
At the same curbside,
      a cast-off cabinet
Of wavily-warped
      unseasoned wood
Waits to be trundled
      in the trash-man's truck.
Haul them off! Hide them!
      The heart winces
For junk and gimcrack,
      for jerrybuilt things
And the men who make them
      for a little money,
Bartering pride
      like the bought boxer
Who pulls his punches,
      or the paid-off jockey
Who in the home stretch
      holds in his horse.

Yet the things themselves
                    in thoughtless honor
Have kept composure,
                    like captives who would not
Talk under torture.
            Tossed from a tailgate
Where the dump displays
                    its random dolmens,
Its black barrows
            and blazing valleys,
They shall waste in the weather
                    toward what they were.
The sun shall glory
            in the glitter of glass-chips,
Foreseeing the salvage
                    of the prisoned sand,
And the blistering paint
                    peel off in patches,
That the good grain
            be discovered again.
Then burnt, bulldozed,
            they shall all be buried
To the depth of diamonds,
                    in the making dark
Where halt Hephaestus
            keeps his hammer
And Wayland's work
            is worn away.

RICHARD WILBUR

JUNK: *The epigraph, taken from a fragmentary Anglo-Saxon poem,
concerns the legendary smith Wayland, and may roughly be translated:
"Truly, Wayland's handiwork—the sword Mimming which he made—will
never fail any man who knows how to use it bravely."—R. W.*

Dulcimer Maker

Calf-deep in spruce dust,
wood curls off his knife,
blade wet, bare bulb light.

The finish of his hands
shows oil, grain, knots
where his growth scarred him.

Planing black oak
thin to flow sounds.
Tones of wind filling
bottle lips.

It is his work tying strings
across fresh-cut pine.

He sings into wood, listens:
tree rings, water!

The wood drinks his cloth,
its roots going to the depths of him,
spreading.

He wants to build a lute for music
carved on Sumerian stones, a music
no one has heard for three thousand years.

For this he will work
the oldest wood he can find.
It will not be as far away,
as unfamiliar.

CAROLYN FORCHÉ

The Young Glass-Stainer

"These Gothic windows, how they wear me out
With cusp and foil, and nothing straight or square,
Crude colours, leaden borders roundabout,
And fitting in Peter here, and Matthew there!

"What a vocation! Here do I draw now
The abnormal, loving the Hellenic norm;
Martha I paint, and dream of Hera's brow,
Mary, and think of Aphrodite's form."

THOMAS HARDY

The Byfield Rabbit

These white-clay pits of Byfield—
Small, intensively worked—
Scarcely disturbed the grass,
The woods not at all. There,
Shadows changed the kilns
To grossly chimneyed castles,
Suitable for dwarves.

Summer, you'd see the wheels
Outside the huts, lugged
Under the lark-strewn sky
Where light winds plied the meadow.
Then wheel-whir, bee-hum, bird-song
In single sound arose,
And fell, like oars in water.

The clay renowned, the potters
For vases, birds and small
Familial animals.
A Byfield Rabbit was
A term for excellence.
You'd think young princesses,
But grown men collected them.

Stranger, repose yourself
On tufted sun-warmed grass
And think of watery sound
Until it's spread so wide
A rabbit rushes by you.
His own ears quivered back,
Stare-eyed, stretched-out-skinny,
Rab runs a vanished course
Of potters treadling clay;
Clay his great-great-grandsire
Leaped into and there,
Enporcelained, became
A term for excellence.

KATHERINE HOSKINS

Hazardous Occupations

Jugglers keep six bottles in the air.
Club swingers toss up six and eight.
The knife throwers miss each other's
    ears by a hair and the steel quivers
    in the target wood.
The trapeze battlers do a back-and-forth
    high in the air with a girl's feet
    and ankles upside down.
So they earn a living—till they miss
    once, twice, even three times.
So they live on hate and love as gipsies
    live in satin skins and shiny eyes.
In their graves do the elbows jostle once
    in a blue moon—and wriggle to throw
    a kiss answering a dreamed-of applause?
Do the bones repeat: It's a *good* act—
    we got a *good* hand . . . .?

CARL SANDBURG

The Policeman's Lot

When a felon's not engaged in his employment,
   Or maturing his felonious little plans,
His capacity for innocent enjoyment
   Is just as great as any honest man's.
Our feelings we with difficulty smother
   When constabulary duty's to be done:
Ah, take one consideration with another,
   A policeman's lot is not a happy one!

When the enterprising burglar's not a-burgling,
   When the cut-throat isn't occupied in crime,
He loves to hear the little brook a-gurgling,
   And listen to the merry village chime.
When the coster's finished jumping on his mother,
   He loves to lie a-basking in the sun:
Ah, take one consideration with another,
   The policeman's lot is not a happy one!

W. S. GILBERT
From The Pirates of Penzance

The Toy-Maker

I am the Toy-maker; I have brought from the town
As much in my plack as should fetch a whole crown,
I'll array for you now my stock of renown
And man's the raree will show you.

Here's a horse that is rearing to bound through the smoke
Of cannon and musket, and, face to that ruck,
The horseman with sword ready held for the stroke,
Lord Lucan, maybe, or Prince Charlie.

An old woman sitting and waiting for call,
With her baskets of cockles and apples and all;
A one-legged sailor attending a ball,
And a tailor and nailer busy.

Or would you have these? A goose ganging by,
With head up in challenge to all who come nigh;
A cock with a comb dangling over his eye,
And a hen on a clutch nicely sitting;

Or a duck that is chasing a quick thing around,
Or a crow that is taking three hops on the ground,
Or an ass with head down (he is held in a pound);
Or a fox with his tail curled around him?

A ship made of shells that have sheen of the sea,
All ready to sail for black Barbarie,
The Lowlands of Holland, or High Germanie—
And who'll be the one that will steer her?

I'll speak of my trade: there's a day beyond day
When the hound needn't hunt and the priest needn't pray,
And the clerk needn't write, and the hen needn't lay,
Whence come all the things that I show you.

I am the Toy-maker; upon the town wall
My crib is high up; I have down-look on all,
And coach and wheelbarrow I carve in my stall,
Making things with no troubles in them.

PADRAIC COLUM

Rich man
Poor man
Beggar man
Thief
Doctor
Lawyer
Indian Chief

AMERICAN NURSERY RHYME

Tinker,
Tailor,
Soldier,
Sailor,
Gentleman,
Apothecary,
Plough-boy,
Thief.

Soldier brave, sailor true,
Skilled physician, Oxford blue,
Learned lawyer, squire so hale,
Dashing airman, curate pale.

Army, Navy,
Medicine, Law,
Church, Nobility,
Nothing at all.

ENGLISH NURSERY RHYMES

A laird, a lord,
A cooper, a thief,
A piper, a drummer,
A stealer of beef.

SCOTTISH NURSERY RHYME

old people working (garden, car)

Old people working. Making a gift of garden.
Or washing a car, so some one else may ride.
A note of alliance, an eloquence of pride.
A way of greeting or sally to the world.

GWENDOLYN BROOKS

The Lamplighter

My tea is nearly ready and the sun has left the sky;
It's time to take the window to see Leerie going by;
For every night at tea-time and before you take your seat,
With lantern and with ladder he comes posting up the street.

Now Tom would be a driver and Maria go to sea,
And my papa's a banker and as rich as he can be;
But I, when I am stronger and can choose what I'm to do,
O Leerie, I'll go round at night and light the lamps with you!

For we are very lucky, with a lamp before the door,
And Leerie stops to light it as he lights so many more;
And O! before you hurry by with ladder and with light,
O Leerie, see a little child and nod to him to-night!

ROBERT LOUIS STEVENSON

Index to Authors

Index to Titles

[166]

[168]

Red brick building, 70
Rich man, 158

She sweeps with many-colored Brooms, 47
She wasn't the least bit pretty, 64
Sighing high and, 67
Skilled to pull wires, he baffles Nature's, 105
Some are teethed on a silver spoon, 82
Something goes wrong with my synthetic brain, 92
Some whirled scythes through the thick oats, 16
Summer is gone and all the merry noise, 25
"Surely there is a mine for silver, 90

That hump of a man bunching chrysanthemums, 19
The hand that arches for the pitchfork heft, 29
Their fingers numb in the thimbles, 50
The labouring poor, in spite of double pay, 81
The lady director is a gentle guide. But, 56
The lariat snaps; the cowboy rolls, 12
The pigeons that peck at the grass in Trinity Churchyard, 112
"These Gothic windows, how they wear me out, 151
These, in the day when heaven was falling, 134
These white-clay pits of Byfield, 152
The soft grey of the distant hills, 68
The swinging mill bell changed its rate, 94
The working girls in the morning are going to, 55
They have been with us a long time, 122
They used to tell me I was building a dream, 107
This ancient hag, 54
Tinker, 159
Twenty men stand watching the muckers, 106

Walking around in the park, 116
We are the desperate, 109
We had expected everything but revolt, 123
When Adam delved and Eve span, 3
When a felon's not engaged in his employment, 155
When for school o'er Little Field with its brook and wooden, 26
When Levin mowed Mashkin Hill, 15
When my mother died I was very young, 86
When there are minds to heal, and you, 43
Where he stood in boots in water to his calves, 132
Who can find a virtuous woman? for her price is, 35
Who decided what is useful in its beauty, 44
Why shall I keep the old name?, 113
With fingers weary and worn, 38

Acknowledgments

*Permission to reprint copyrighted poems is
gratefully acknowledged to the following:*

Atheneum Publishers, Inc., for "Iowa Land" from *Residue of Song* by Marvin Bell,
Copyright © 1974 by Marvin Bell; "Application for a Grant" from *The Venetian
Vespers* by Anthony Hecht, Copyright © 1979 by Anthony Hecht; and "The
Byfield Rabbit" from *Excursions, New & Selected Poems* by Katherine Hoskins,
Copyright © 1966 by Katherine Hoskins.

Ben Belitt, for "Charwoman" from *The Enemy Joy* by Ben Belitt (University of
Chicago Press, 1964), Copyright © 1964 by Ben Belitt.

Brandt & Brandt Literary Agents, Inc., for "Nightmare Number Three" by Stephen
Vincent Benét from *The Selected Works of Stephen Vincent Benét,* Holt, Rinehart,
and Winston, Inc., Copyright, 1937, by Stephen Vincent Benét, Copyright renewed
© 1964, by Thomas C. Benét, Stephanie B. Mahin, and Rachel Benét Lewis.

John Malcolm Brinnin, for "Girl in a White Coat" and "With a Posthumous
Medal" from *No Arch No Triumph,* Copyright 1945 by John Malcolm Brinnin.

Malcolm Cowley, for "The Hill Above the Mine" from *Blue Juniata: Collected
Poems,* Copyright © 1968 by Malcom Cowley.

The Devin-Adair Co., Old Greenwich, Conn. 06870, for "The Toy-maker" and
"The Knitters" from *The Collected Poems of Padraic Colum,* Copyright 1953 by
Padraic Colum, renewed 1981.

Doubleday & Company, Inc., for "Song of the Weaving Woman" by Yuan Chen,
translated by Wu-chi Liu, "Weaving at the Window" by Wang Chien, translated by
William H. Nienhauser, and "An Old Charcoal Seller" by Po Chu-yi, translated by
Eugene Eoyang, all from *Sunflower Splendor,* co-edited by Wu-chi Liu and Irving
Yucheng Lo, Copyright © 1975 by Wu-chi Liu and Irving Lo; "Frau Bauman, Frau
Schmidt, and Frau Schwartze" from *The Collected Poems of Theodore Roethke,*
Copyright 1952 by Theodore Roethke (originally in *The New Yorker*); and "Old
Florist" from *The Collected Poems of Theodore Roethke* by Theodore Roethke,
Copyright 1946 by Harper & Brothers.

Hyman Eigerman, for poems 21 and 44 from *The Poetry of Dorothy Wordsworth,*
edited by Hyman Eigerman, Copyright © 1940 by Columbia University Press.

Norma Millay Ellis, for "Men Working" and an excerpt from "Journal" by Edna St.
Vincent Millay from *Collected Poems,* Harper & Row, Copyright © 1954 by
Norma Millay (Ellis).

Faber and Faber Ltd., for "Toads Revisited" from *The Whitsun Weddings,* by
Philip Larkin, Copyright © 1964 by Philip Larkin.

[171]

[172]

Macmillan Press Ltd., for "You on the Tower" and "The Young Glass-Stainer" from *Complete Poems of Thomas Hardy*, edited by James Gibson (Canadian rights only).

Macmillan Publishing Co., Inc., for "You on the Tower" and "The Young Glass-Stainer" from *Complete Poems of Thomas Hardy*, edited by James Gibson.

Ellen C. Masters, for "Butch Weldy" and "Cooney Potter" from *Spoon River Anthology* by Edgar Lee Masters; and "Willis Beggs" from *The New Spoon River* by Edgar Lee Masters, Macmillan Publishing Co., Inc.

William Morrow & Company, Inc., for "Mashkin Hill" from *Searching for the Ox* by Louis Simpson, Copyright © 1976 by Louis Simpson.

National Council of the Churches of Christ in the United States of America, for Job 28: 1-4 and 9-11 from the *Revised Standard Version of the Bible*, Copyright 1946, 1952, © 1971, 1973.

New Directions Publishing Corp., for "Le Médecin Malgré Lui" from *The Collected Earlier Poems* by William Carlos Williams, Copyright 1938 by New Directions Publishing Corporation.

W. W. Norton & Company, Inc., for "Boulder Dam" and "Prayer Before Work" from *Collected Poems, 1930–1973*, by May Sarton, Copyright © 1974 by May Sarton.

The Ohio University Press, Athens, for "The Gnomes" from *Phone Calls From the Dead* by Beth Bentley.

The Overlook Press, Lewis Hollow Road, Woodstock, N.Y. 12498, for "That Day" from *I Remember Root River* by David Kherdian, Copyright © 1978 by David Kherdian.

Persea Books, Inc., for "The Closing of the Rodeo" from *The Traveler's Tree, New and Selected Poems*, by William Jay Smith, Copyright © 1980 by William Jay Smith.

Princeton University Press, for "You Owe Them Everything" from *Walking Four Ways in the Wind* by John Allman, Copyright © 1979 by Princeton University Press; and "Huswifery" from *The Poetical Works of Edward Taylor*, edited and with an Introduction and Notes by Thomas H. Johnson, Copyright 1939 by Rockland, 1943 by Princeton University Press.

Random House, Inc., for "Song for the Old Ones" and "Southeast Arkanasia" from *Oh Pray My Wings Are Gonna Fit Me Well* by Maya Angelou, Copyright © 1975 by Maya Angelou; Section 1 of "Sext," Copyright © 1955 by W. H. Auden, from *W. H. Auden: Collected Poems*, edited by Edward Mendelson; "The Outwit Song" from *The Center of Attention* by Daniel Hoffman, Copyright © 1974 by Daniel Hoffman; and 5 lines from "Boys Will, Joyful Labor Without Pay, and Harvest Home (1918)," Copyright © 1957 by Robert Penn Warren, from *Selected Poems, 1923-1975*, by Robert Penn Warren.

Jane Smith, for "The Song of a Factory Worker" by Ruth Collins; "Dawn" by Constance Ortmayer; and "A Factory Rainbow" by Rose Saadi.

The Society of Authors, as the literary representative of the Estate of A.E.

Housman, and Jonathan Cape Ltd., publishers of A.E. Housman's *Collected Poems,* for "Epitaph on an Army of Mercenaries" from *The Collected Poems of A.E. Housman* (Canadian rights only).

The University of Illinois Press, for the poems from *The Factory Girls,* edited by Philip S. Foner, on pages 58-65.

University of Missouri Press and Willis Barnstone, for "Changsha Shoe Factory" from *China Poems* by Willis Barnstone, Copyright © 1976 by Willis Barnstone.

Viking Penguin Inc., for "Trinity Place" from *Times Three* by Phyllis McGinley, Copyright 1937 by Phyllis McGinley, © renewed 1965 by Phyllis McGinley; and "The Case for the Miners" from *Collected Poems* by Siegfried Sassoon, published by The Viking Press in 1949.

Warner Bros. Music, for "Brother Can You Spare a Dime" by E. Y. Harburg and Jay Gorney, © 1932 (Renewed) Warner Bros., Inc., All Rights Reserved. Used by Permission.

Wesleyan University Press, for "Tiempo Muerto" from *Cimmaron* by Ricardo Alonso, Copyright © 1979 by Ricardo Alonso.

Yale University Press, for "Dulcimer Maker" from *Gathering the Tribes* by Carolyn Forché, Copyright © 1976 by Carolyn Forché.

My thanks to Carole Forman for her expert secretarial help. And my thanks to Fannie Turkel and to Helen Abrams for their help in finding the poems by the working women of the nineteenth century.
    —H. P.